2

College Oral
Communication

College Oral Communication

2

HOUGHTON MIFFLIN
ENGLISH FOR ACADEMIC SUCCESS

Ann E. Roemer

Utah State University

SERIES EDITORS

Patricia Byrd

Joy M. Reid

Cynthia M. Schuemann

Houghton Mifflin Company

Boston   New York

Publisher: Patricia A. Coryell
Director of ESL Publishing: Susan Maguire
Senior Development Editor: Kathy Sands Boehmer
Editorial Assistant: Evangeline Bermas
Senior Project Editor: Kathryn Dinovo
Manufacturing Assistant: Karmen Chong
Senior Marketing Manager: Annamarie Rice

Cover graphics: LMA Communications, Natick, Massachusetts

Photo Credits: © Owen Franken/Corbis, p. 1; © Arthur Morris/Corbis, p. 35; © George D. Lepp/ Corbis, p. 36; © Sergio Pitamitz/Corbis, p. 37, top; © David Samuel Robbins/Corbis, p. 37, center; © Gary Braasch/Corbis, p. 37, bottom; © Royalty Free/Corbis, p. 38, both; © Gavriel Jecan/Corbis, p. 50; © Sandro Vannini, p. 73; © Roger Ressmeyer/Corbis, p.109; © Getty Images, p. 110, left; © Alison Wright/Corbis, p. 110, right; © Jim Craigmyle/Corbis, p.152; © Royalty Free/Corbis, p. 154, top left; © Reuters/Corbis, p. 154, top right; © Tom Nebbia/ Corbis, p. 154, bottom left; © Dale C. Spartas/Corbis, p. 154, bottom right; © Royalty Free/ Corbis, p. 173; © Dainna Sarto/Corbis, p. 191.

Printed in the U.S.A.

Library of Congress Control Number: 2004112209

ISBN: 0-618-23017-3

123456789-CRW-08 07 06 05 04

Contents

Houghton Mifflin English for Academic Success Series

SERIES EDITORS

Patricia Byrd, Joy M. Reid, Cynthia M. Schuemann

▷ What Is the Purpose of This Series?

The Houghton Mifflin English for Academic Success series is a comprehensive program of student and instructor materials: four levels of student language proficiency textbooks in three skill areas (oral communication, reading, and writing), with supplemental vocabulary textbooks at each level. For instructors and students, a useful website supports classroom teaching, learning, and assessment. For instructors, four Essentials of Teaching Academic Language books (*Essentials of Teaching Academic Oral Communication, Essentials of Teaching Academic Reading, Essentials of Teaching Academic Writing,* and *Essentials of Teaching Academic Vocabulary*) provide helpful information for instructors new to teaching oral communication, reading, writing, and vocabulary.

The fundamental purpose of the series is to prepare students who are not native speakers of English for academic success in U.S. college degree programs. By studying these materials, students in college English for Academic Purposes (EAP) courses will gain the academic language skills they need to be successful students in degree programs. Additionally, students will learn about being successful students in U.S. college courses.

The series is based on considerable prior research, as well as our own investigations of students' needs and interests, instructors' needs and desires, and institutional expectations and requirements. For example, our survey research revealed what problems instructors feel they face in their classrooms and what they actually teach; who the students are and what they know and do not know about the "culture" of U.S. colleges; and what types of exams are required for admission at various colleges.

Student Audience

The materials in this series are for college-bound ESL students at U.S. community colleges and undergraduate programs at other institutions. Some of these students are U.S. high school graduates. Some of them are long-term U.S. residents who graduated from a high school before coming to the United States. Others are newer U.S. residents. Still others are more typical international students. All of them need to develop academic language skills and knowledge of ways to be successful in U.S. college degree courses.

All of the books in this series have been created to implement the Houghton Mifflin English for Academic Success competencies. These competencies are based on those developed by ESL instructors and administrators in Florida, California, and Connecticut to be the underlying structure for EAP courses at colleges in those states. These widely respected competencies assure that the materials meet the real-world needs of EAP students and instructors.

All of the books focus on . . .

► Starting where the students are, building on their strengths and prior knowledge (which is considerable, if not always academically relevant), and helping students self-identify needs and plans to strengthen academic language skills

► Academic English, including development of Academic Vocabulary and grammar required by students for academic speaking/listening, reading, and writing

► Master Student Skills, including learning-style analysis, strategy training, and learning about the "culture" of U.S. colleges, which lead to their becoming successful students in degree courses and degree programs

► Topics and readings that represent a variety of academic disciplinary areas so that students learn about the language and content of the social sciences, the hard sciences, education, and business as well as the humanities

All of the books provide . . .

► Interesting and valuable content that helps the students develop their knowledge of academic content as well as their language skills and student skills

► A wide variety of practical classroom-tested activities that are easy to teach and engage the students

► Assessment tools at the end of each chapter so that instructors have easy-to-implement ways to assess student learning and students have opportunities to assess their own growth

► Websites for the students and for the instructors: the student sites will provide additional opportunities to practice reading, writing, listening, vocabulary development, and grammar. The instructor sites will provide instructor's manuals, teaching notes and answer keys, value-added materials like handouts and overheads that can be reproduced to use in class, and assessment tools such as additional tests to use beyond the assessment materials in each book.

▷ What Is the Purpose of the Oral Communication Strand?

The Oral Communication strand of Houghton Mifflin English for Academic Success focuses on development of speaking and listening skills necessary for college study. Dedicated to meeting academic needs of students by teaching them how to handle the spoken English used by instructors and students in college classrooms, the four books provide engaging activities to practice both academic listening and academic speaking. Students learn to participate effectively in a variety of academic situations, including discussions, lectures, student study groups, and office meetings with their college instructors.

Because of the importance of academic vocabulary in the spoken English of the classroom, the oral communication strand teaches the students techniques for learning and using new academic vocabulary both to recognize the words when they hear them and to use the words in their own spoken English. Grammar appropriate to the listening and speaking activities is also included in each chapter. For example, Book 2 includes work with the pronunciation of irregular past tense verbs as part of learning how to talk with a professor about a problem. In addition to language development, the books provide for academic skill development through the teaching of appropriate academic tasks and the giving of "master student" tips to help students better understand what is expected of them in college classes. Students learn to carry out academic tasks in ways that are linguistically, academically, and culturally appropriate. For example, students learn how to take information from the spoken presentations by their instructors and then to use that information for other academic tasks such as tests or small group discussions. That is, students are not taught to take notes for some abstract reason but learn to make a powerful connection between note-taking and success in other assigned tasks.

Each book has a broad disciplinary theme to give coherence to the content. These themes were selected because of their high interest for students; they are also topics commonly explored in introductory college courses and so provide useful background for students. Materials were selected that are academically appropriate but that do not require expert knowledge by the instructor. The following themes are used: Book 1: Human Psychology, Book 2: The Connections between Human Beings and Animals, Book 3: Communication and Media, and Book 4: Money. For example, Book 1 has one chapter about the psychological effects of music and another on the relationship between nutrition and psychological well-being. Book 2 uses topics such as taboo foods, dogs as workers, the scientific method (using mice in mazes for psychology experiments about learning), along with Aesop's fables. Book 3 includes the history of movies, computer animation, privacy rights, and other topics related to modern media. Book 4 takes on a topic that fascinates most students with various themes related to money, including such related topics as the history of money, marketing use of psychological conditioning, and the economics of the World Wide Web. These topics provide high-interest content for use in the listening and speaking activities, but do not require that instructors have to develop any new knowledge to be able to use the materials.

Instructor Support Materials

Recorded materials presented in each chapter are available on an audiotape or CD that is provided with each book. In addition to a recording of the main lecture for each chapter, the recording includes other materials such as dialogues and academic vocabulary.

The series also includes a resource book for instructors called *Essentials of Teaching Academic Oral Communication* by John Murphy. This practical book provides strategies and activities for instructors new to the teaching of oral communication.

▷ What Is the Organization of *College Oral Communication 2*?

College Oral Communication 2 prepares intermediate-level students for the demands of college-level academic speaking and listening tasks. Five chapters of lectures in humanities, natural science, nutrition and social sciences, math and business, and animal science present concepts and language that many students will encounter in future college courses.

Vocabulary is a prominent feature of the textbook. Each chapter provides a list of academic words related to the lecture, supported by pronunciation work in syllable number and stress.

Master Student Tips scattered throughout the textbook provide students with short comments on a particular strategy, activity, or practical advice to follow in an academic setting.

Chapter Organization

Each chapter is clearly divided into three sections: Effective Academic Listening, Effective Academic Speaking, and Assessing Your Academic Speaking and Listening Skills.

Effective Academic Listening

Getting Ready for the Lecture Readings, charts, and tables engage students in the content and prepare them to listen and take notes from lectures. Note-taking strategies such as recognizing signal words for different patterns of organization, using symbols and abbreviations, and working with content vocabulary prepare students to listen and take notes from academic lectures and classroom communication.

Getting Information from the Lecture Students are guided toward successful note-taking by predicting content and organization. Students listen to academic lectures and use provided outlines as models of effective note-taking.

Understanding Teacher Talk Teachers make announcements about office hours, quizzes, assignments, etc.—information that ESL students often miss. In this section of the chapter, Understanding Teacher Talk, students learn to be aware of expressions and gestures that professors use to convey important information.

Using Your Lecture Notes Book 2 guides students through the note-taking process, beginning with an examination of sample notes and a discussion of the features of good lecture notes. They practice using common abbreviations and symbols, and are gradually led to taking notes independently on longer listening passages. Two methods of note-taking are taught: outlining and concept mapping. In later chapters, when taking notes on their own, students choose the method they prefer.

Students participate in academic tasks directly related to their notes and the content of the particular chapter. Tasks include preparing an oral summary, predicting test questions, making study aids such as graphic organizers or concept cards, and using notes to synthesize lecture and reading content.

Effective Academic Speaking

Activities in this section all resemble types of academic tasks expected of students in the college environment such as taking on roles and participating in small-group discussions on lecture content, case studies, or personal experiences, presenting oral summaries, giving short presentations, providing feedback to classmates' presentations, talking on the telephone, and leaving effective voicemail messages.

Power Grammar Each chapter in Book 2 has two–three Academic Speaking Tasks. Prior to each of these, students learn the language they need to perform the task successfully. In addition to vocabulary and pronunciation, important grammar is explained in a section called Power Grammar. For example, as a prelude to the academic task of describing graphs and charts, students review numbers in English, including decimals, and in the Power Grammar box they study forms of the comparative and superlative. They are then asked to use this vocabulary and grammar to complete the Academic Speaking Task.

Assessing Your Speaking and Listening Skills

Additional academic listening and speaking and note-taking tasks are provided with similar content material to allow students to demonstrate that they have mastered the objectives of the chapter. In addition, students are given the opportunity to reflect on several of the academic strategies they learned and practiced in the chapter. Each chapter ends with a listing of the chapter objectives for students to evaluate their progress.

Acknowledgments

This textbook is the result of the hard work, dedication, determination, and collaboration of numerous people. Susan Maguire's ESL team at Houghton Mifflin, in particular, Kathy Sands Boehmer, supported me in this endeavor, both professionally and personally. The unending energy, patience, and encouragement of Pat What-Can-I-Do-to-Help Byrd, series editor, inspired me, along with the camaraderie and counsel of my fellow Oral Communication authors, Marsha Chan, Cheryl Delk, and Steve Jones. My forthright advisory group of teachers from Salt Lake Community College—Maryos Kuiper, Donna Mirabelli, and Vicky Wason—were indispensable in the revision process. More revisions ensued with constructive comments from Sarina Chugani-Molina, Palomar College; Laurie Berry Cox, Midlands Technical Community College; Cheryl Delk, Georgia State University; Timothy Ely, Harcum College; Robert Giron, Montgomery College; Pamela Kennedy, Holyoke Community College; Genevieve Lau, Skyline College; Pauline Pharr, Suffolk County Community College; Janine Rudnick, El Paso Community College; Pamela Sherman, Ulster Community College; Shirley Terrell, Collin County Community College; Anastassia Tzoytzoyrakos, University of Southern California; Hoda Zaki, Camden County College; and Kathy Zuo, William Rainey Harper College.

I am grateful to my extraordinary colleagues and students in the Intensive English Language Institute at Utah State University, who sustained my sanity and sense of humor during most trying times.

This book is dedicated to Florence Bertram Roemer (1912–2003) and Stewart Allen (1938–2003).

▷ What Student Competencies Are Covered in *College Oral Communication 2*?

Houghton Mifflin English for Academic Success Competencies

College Oral Communication 2

Description of Overall Purposes

Students continue to develop speaking and listening skills necessary for participating in classroom discussions with an introduction to oral presentation and critical listening skills.

With the Materials in This Book, a Student Will Learn:

Production

Competency 1: The student will participate in classroom discussion, express opinions, and be understood by attentive listeners. The student will continue to develop oral communication skills including fluency, idea sequencing, accuracy, vocabulary, and pronunciation. The student will learn about and develop a few strategies for helping others to understand her or him.

Competency 2: The student will ask informational questions and ask for clarification.

Competency 3: The student will actively participate in role-playing, simulating academic situations (e.g., asking questions during an instructor's lecture, expressing opinions, stating data and factual information, and drawing conclusions).

Competency 4: The student will prepare simple oral presentations on familiar topics (e.g., comparison, classification, process).

Comprehension

Competency 5: The student will follow orally expressed multistep directions appropriate to the level.

Competency 6: The student will understand factual information and respond appropriately to comprehension questions.

Competency 7: The student will take notes on contemporary topics (e.g., news items, reports). The student will use the notes for academically appropriate purposes such as preparing for a test or for a classroom presentation.

▷ What Are the Features of the Oral Communication Books?

The Houghton Mifflin English for Academic Success series is a comprehensive program of student and instructor materials. The fundamental purpose of the program is to prepare students who are not native speakers of English for academic success in U.S. college degree programs.

The Oral Communication strand of the Houghton Mifflin English for Academic Success series focuses on development of speaking and listening skills necessary for college study. Dedicated to meeting academic needs of students by teaching them how to handle the spoken English used by instructors and students in college classrooms, the four books provide engaging activities to practice both academic listening and academic speaking. Students learn to participate effectively in a variety of academic situations, including discussions, lectures, study groups, and office meetings with their college instructors.

Broad Disciplinary Themes: Each book has a broad disciplinary theme to give coherence to the content. These themes were selected because of their high interest for students. They are also topics commonly explored in introductory college courses and so provide useful background for students.

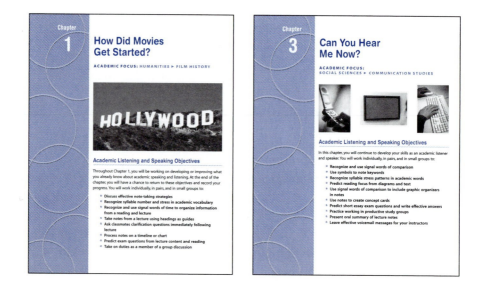

Effective Academic Listening: Students listen to authentic classroom interactions and lectures. They learn to take information from the spoken presentations and use their notes for other academic tasks such as tests or small group discussions.

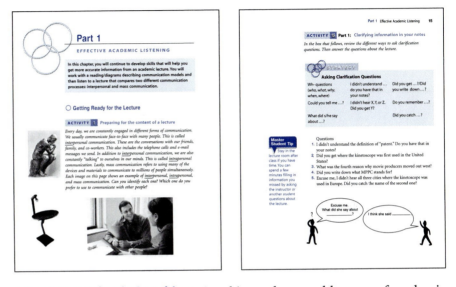

Effective Academic Speaking: Speaking tasks resemble types of academic tasks expected of students in the college environment. These speaking tasks include taking on roles and participating in small group formal and informal discussions on lecture content, presenting oral summaries, and leaving effective voicemail messages. Students learn to do oral presentations appropriate to their proficiency level and to college study.

Self-Assessment of Academic Speaking and Listening Skills: Students are given the opportunity to reflect on several of the academic strategies they learned and practiced in the chapters. Each chapter ends with a listing of the chapter objectives for students to evaluate their progress.

Academic Vocabulary: The Oral Communication strand teaches students techniques for learning and using new academic vocabulary in order to recognize the words when they hear them and to also use the words in their own spoken English.

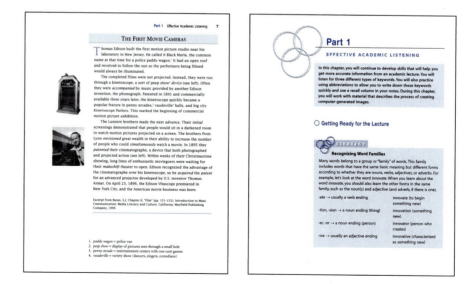

Academic Listening and Speaking Strategies: Key strategies and skills are interspersed throughout each book. Students can clearly see important concepts to focus on as they complete the activities in each chapter. Highlighted strategies will help students improve both their listening and speaking skills.

Master Student Tips: Master Student Tips throughout the textbooks provide students with short comments on a particular strategy, activity, or practical advice to follow in an academic setting. Instructors can use these tips to help students become better students by building their understanding of college study.

Power Grammar Boxes: Students can be very diverse in their grammar and rhetorical needs so each chapter contains Power Grammar boxes that introduce the grammar structures students need to be fluent and accurate in academic English.

Ancillary Program: The following items are available to accompany the Houghton Mifflin English for Academic Success Series Oral Communication strand.

► Instructor Website: Additional teaching materials, activities, and robust student assessment.

► Student Website: Additional exercises and activities.

► Audio Program: Available on either CD-ROM or cassette.

► The Houghton Mifflin English for Academic Success series Vocabulary books: You can choose the appropriate level to shrinkwrap with your text.

► *Essentials of Teaching Academic Oral Communication* by John Murphy is available for purchase. It gives you theoretical and practical information for teaching oral communication.

1

Cry Wolf

ACADEMIC FOCUS: HUMANITIES

Academic Listening and Speaking Objectives

In this chapter, you will work individually, in pairs, and in small groups to:

- ► Learn about Aesop's fables
- ► Find countries on a map of the world
- ► Listen for word and sentence stress
- ► Recognize good lecture notes and the difference between notes and dictation
- ► Listen for definitions in a humanities lecture
- ► Listen for main ideas and details in a lecture
- ► Use a dictionary to pronounce new words
- ► Ask questions about language: meaning, pronunciation, and spelling
- ► Participate in class discussions, using verbal and nonverbal communication

Part 1

EFFECTIVE ACADEMIC LISTENING

This chapter's lecture, "Cry Wolf," comes from the humanities, areas of study related to human thought and culture. Sometimes called *liberal arts*, humanities courses are required at colleges and universities as part of a student's general education.

▷ Getting Ready for the Lecture

ACTIVITY 1 Using a map

To get ready for this chapter's humanities lecture, discuss the following questions in your group.

1. Look at the world map. Where do you live? Where is your family from? Find the country on the map and show your classmates.
2. What countries have you traveled to? What countries are in the news? Find them on the map.
3. Find Greece on the map. Why is Greece important in the humanities?
4. Look at the following titles of stories. Do you recognize any of them? If so, tell the story to your group. If not, can you think of another story that you are familiar with?

Little Red Riding Hood	Hodja stories
Old Man Yu Moves Mountains	Simchung
The Emperor's New Clothes	Cinderella
Scheherazade and the Tales of 1001 Nights	Momotaro
The City Mouse and the Country Mouse	The Fox and the Grapes

5. As a group, choose one of the stories and share it with the rest of the class.

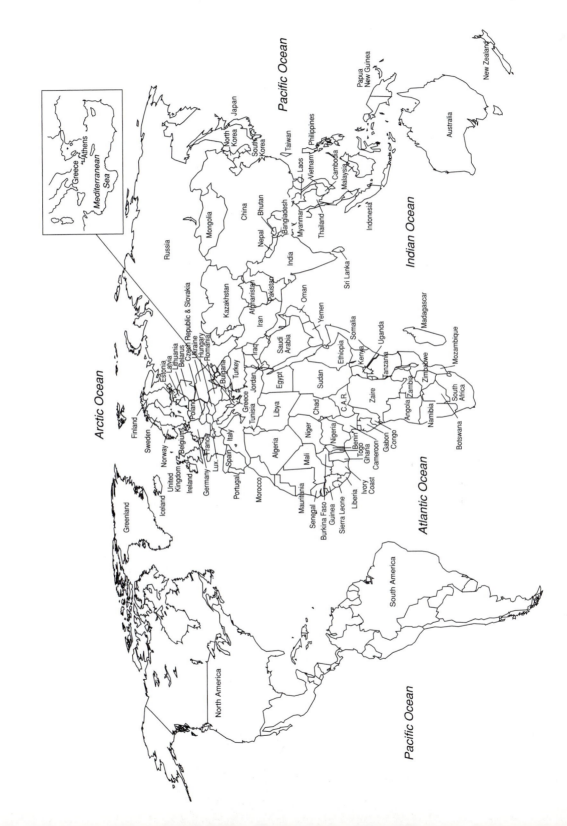

Notes vs. Dictation

Students need to take notes while they listen to their instructors' lectures. Because ESL students have written dictations in their language classes, they sometimes confuse "taking notes" with "writing a dictation." This chart contrasts notes and dictations to help you become a better academic listener. Notes are not like a dictation. They look different and they are used differently. This chart contrasts notes and dictations.

Notes	Dictation
Ideas are important.	Form is important (correct spelling, capitalization).
Not everything is included—only important ideas.	Every word is included.
Abbreviations and symbols are used to represent ideas. There's no time to write complete words and sentences!	Complete sentences are used.
The purpose of notes: to help you remember ideas that you heard.	The purpose of a dictation: to evaluate your listening comprehension and writing in a language class.
If you miss part of a lecture, you can leave a space and fill in the information later.	If you miss part of a dictation, you fail that part.
Notes are personal; they are for you, the student, so it's important that you understand them, especially a couple of weeks after you take them.	A dictation is for you and the instructor to see how well you understand spoken English and write the words you hear.
Sample notes: West. civ. from Greece	**Sample dictation:** What we know as Western civilization originates, or comes from, ancient Greece.

ACTIVITY 2   **Identifying notes vs. dictation**

Look through Part 1 of this chapter and find five examples of notes and two examples of a dictation. Compare your answers with your partner's.

Notes found on pages _____

Dictation found on pages _____

POWER GRAMMAR

Different Uses of *Or*

The word *or* has more than one meaning. The first is to show different possibilities: *hot or cold*, and the second is to give a definition, or synonym. Professors often use *or* with the second meaning, because they use new words in their lectures that the students need to learn.

ACTIVITY 3   **Listening for definitions**

Listen to the following excerpts from the lecture, and write the synonym, or definition, that the lecturer gives for the following words.

> **You hear:** The topic of today's lecture is from the humanities, or subjects such as art, literature, and philosophy.
>
> **You write:** *the humanities:* subjects such as art, literature, and philosophy

1. *originates:* _____

2. *pass on:* _____

3. *moral:* _____

4. *cried:* _____

5. *illustrates:* _____

Listening for Sentence Stress

Taking notes is one of the most important skills that college students need. Professors lecture, or speak, and students are expected to listen and write the important ideas from the lecture. These ideas are often stressed; in other words, the professors seem to emphasize, or say some words louder than other words. The stressed syllables in these words sound louder and longer than those in other words. The words are called *content words* because they contain the important ideas. They are often nouns (*Aesop, fable*), verbs (*originates, entertain*), adjectives (*famous*), and adverbs (*orally*).

ACTIVITY **4** **Hearing sentence stress**

*Listen to your instructor and fill in the blanks with the missing content words from the beginning of the lecture. (The stressed syllables of the other content words are in **bold** print.)*

What we _know_ as **West**ern civili**za**tion o**rig**inates, or _____

from, **an**cient _____. One of the most **fam**ous _____,

though we're not even sure if he _____ **lived** or if he was a **myth**,

was **Ae**sop. We **think** that _____ lived around _____ BC.

He was a **slave**, and he is **fam**ous for his _____, which, like **most**

stories, were told **or**ally. **Ae**sop's _____ were not written **down**

until the **cent**ury after he _____.

Words from the Lecture

In every class, you are expected to understand and use certain words that are important in that subject. The professor uses these words in the humanities lecture. You are expected to know what they mean, how they are pronounced, and how to use them.

ACTIVITY 5   Expanding your vocabulary

Match the words from the list with their definitions. Then check your answers by listening to your instructor. Look at #1 as an example.

accurate	century	fairy tale	proverb	slave
advice	character	fool	role	structure
audience	characteristic	liven up	settle	terrified
BC	common sense	myth	shepherd	unique

1. ____*myth*____ An imaginary story, person, or thing.

2. _____ An abbreviation of *before Christ* (in a specified year before the birth of Jesus in the Christian calendar).

3. _____ A person who is owned by and forced to work for sbdy. else. [*sbdy. = somebody*]

4. _____ A period of 100 years.

5. _____ Being the only one of its kind.

6. _____ A feature or quality that distinguishes a person or thing.

7. _____ A story about fairies, magical creatures, or legendary deeds, usually intended for children.

8. _____ 1. Free from errors or mistakes; correct.
2. Exact; precise.

9. _____ To end or resolve: *settle a dispute/argument/disagreement*.

10. _____ Good judgment gained from everyday experience.

11. _____ The readers, listeners, or viewers of a book, radio broadcast, or television program.

12. _____ Opinion about how to solve a problem; guidance.

13. _____ A person in a work of art, such as a novel, play, or movie.

14. _____ A short saying that is used frequently and expresses a basic truth.

15. _____ A person who herds, guards, and takes care of sheep.

16. _____ To make (sthg.) lively, full of life or energy. [*sthg. = something*]

17. _____ Full of terror; frightened; scared.

18. _____ A person who has no judgment or good sense.

Definitions from *The American Heritage ESL Dictionary.* 1998. Houghton Mifflin.

STRATEGY

Pronunciation ▶ Word Stress

All words in English have one or more syllables. A syllable is unit of sound in a word. If a word has more than one syllable, one of the syllables is always stressed, or pronounced a little louder and longer. In the dictionary, this stress is shown with an accent mark (´). Listen to your instructor pronounce the following words:

Examples:		**Dictionary:**	
	*ar*gument		(är′ gyə mənt)
	*ig*nore		(ĭg nôr′)
	*pur*pose		(pûr′ pəs)
	*cul*ture		(kŭl′ chər)
	*com*mon		(kŏm′ ən)

ACTIVITY **6**   **Hearing word stress**

Listen as your instructor pronounces the words from the Activity 5 vocabulary list, and mark the syllable, or part of the word or phrase, that he or she says with more emphasis. Then check your answers with a partner.

ACTIVITY **7**   **Using new vocabulary**

With a partner, practice asking and answering the questions on page 227 (see Appendix 1). Ask the first four questions, while your partner scans the words in Activity 5 for the answers. Then switch.

Example:

Student A (on page 227): *What century were you born in?*

Student B (looking at page 7): *I was born in the twentieth century.*

▷ Getting Information from the Lecture

Note-taking: Listening for Main Ideas and Details

An important part of being a good note-taker is listening for the main ideas of a lecture. All during a lecture, you have to listen to ideas and ask yourself, "Is this important information? Should I write this in my notes?" It's not possible or necessary to write everything the professor says—you need to recognize the difference between important and unimportant information.

 ACTIVITY 8   Listening for main ideas

The first time you listen to the lecture, "Cry Wolf," try to get a general idea of the topic. As you listen, check (✓) the main ideas that the professor talks about. Look at #1 as an example.

1. ancient . . .

   _____ Alexandria   _____ Asia   _✓_ Greece

2. Aesop was . . .

   _____ attractive   _____ a scientist   _____ a slave

3. Aesop is famous for his . . .

   _____ fables   _____ audience   _____ philosophy

4. fables and fairy tales are . . .

   _____ similar   _____ different

5. fables and their . . .

   _____ causes   _____ characteristics   _____ history

ACTIVITY 9 **Listening for details**

Listen to the lecture again, and check (✓) the ideas that the professor discusses.

1. Aesop probably lived . . .

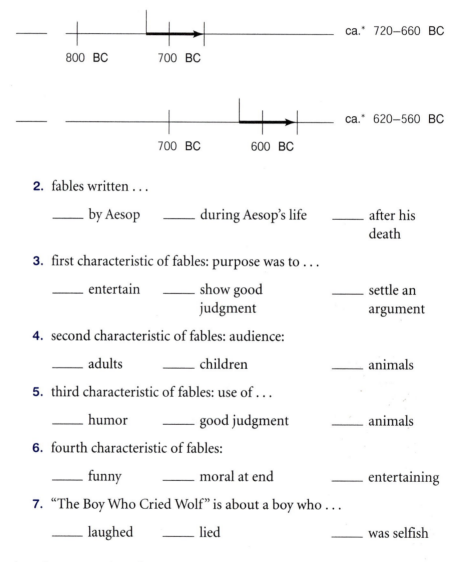

2. fables written . . .

_____ by Aesop   _____ during Aesop's life   _____ after his death

3. first characteristic of fables: purpose was to . . .

_____ entertain   _____ show good judgment   _____ settle an argument

4. second characteristic of fables: audience:

_____ adults   _____ children   _____ animals

5. third characteristic of fables: use of . . .

_____ humor   _____ good judgment   _____ animals

6. fourth characteristic of fables:

_____ funny   _____ moral at end   _____ entertaining

7. "The Boy Who Cried Wolf" is about a boy who . . .

_____ laughed   _____ lied   _____ was selfish

*ca.: circa = approximately

Taking Good Lecture Notes

As the chart on page 4 explains, notes are used for remembering information. In college, questions about this information are often found on tests, so students use their notes to study for tests. Good notes:

► show important ideas from the lecture, written on the far left of the page

► have related ideas written below and to the right of the main ideas

► use abbreviations and symbols to represent meaning

► don't use words such as *the, a, an, is, was, were* . . .

► include what the professor writes on the board

Example:

Good notes

    - imprt. ideas on far left

    - reltd ideas below + right of main ideas

    - use abbrev. + symbols

    - don't use "the, an, . . ."

    - include wht prof puts on brd

ACTIVITY 10   Recognizing good notes

Three students, Li, María, and Jean Marc, listened to the humanities lecture and took the following notes. Look at what they wrote and decide who has the best notes and why. Put a checkmark (✓) next to the best.

_____ **Li's notes:**

Humanities class

- What we know civilization ancient Greece. One famous We think orally.

- Aesop's fables are different from children fairy tales, like Cinderella or Snow White

- This is not an accurate picture.

- settle an argument, pass on common sense. The second characteristic of fables is

- instead of answering, A third characteristic of fables, which

- The animals take on human

- All the stories end The fable you'll hear today

- Once there was young shepherd boy, who watched his sheep

- One afternoon the boy cried, Wolf! Somebody down in the village

- they found the sheep grazing peacefully

- Some time later, thinking that the boy and his sheep were in danger, Again,

- Time passes, the shepherd watched his flock

- Now I'd like you to

_____ **María's notes:**

Aesop's fables

- *Western civilization comes from Greece; one famous Grk maybe myth, was Aesop*

- *600 BC*

- ○

- *3rd characteristic = use of animals*

- *moral*

- *groups of 4 to 5*

_____ **Jean Marc's notes:**

Humanities: Cry wolf

- West. civ. from Greece

    - famous Grk = Aesop, 600 BC?

        ▲ for fables, not written 'til later

- Aesop's fables diff. frm fairy tales

    1. purpose not to entertain, but pass on good judg., settle argument
    2. audience not kids, but adults (fable as advice)
    3. animals as characters
    4. moral @ end = lesson; some now proverbs

- Boy . . . Cried Wolf: shepherd, bored, cries Wolf!

    ▲ villagers go to help, boy laughing, no wolf

    again ⌐

    ▲ wolf really comes, boy cries, no one comes

    ▲ moral: No one likes . . . fool.

- grps, 4–5: how fable illustr. charac. Of Aesop's fable

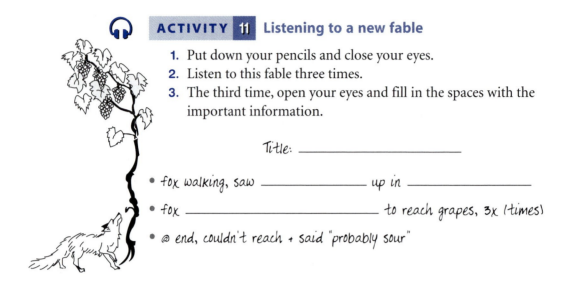

ACTIVITY 11 Listening to a new fable

1. Put down your pencils and close your eyes.
2. Listen to this fable three times.
3. The third time, open your eyes and fill in the spaces with the important information.

Title: _____

• fox walking, saw _____ up in _____

• fox _____ to reach grapes, 3x (times)

• @ end, couldn't reach + said "probably sour"

▷ Recognizing Teacher Talk

In addition to the information in the lecture, professors give information about course requirements such as tests, grades, and assignments, usually at the beginning and/or end of the class. This information is often given orally (it is not written down), and said only once, so you need to listen carefully and write it in your notes.

ACTIVITY 12 Note-taking practice

Listen to the end of the humanities lecture, "Cry Wolf," and take notes about the directions that the professor gives. Then compare the information in your notes with a classmate's.

_____

_____

_____

_____

_____

_____

Using Your Lecture Notes

STRATEGY

Borrowing Notes

If you miss a class lecture, you need to get the information that you missed. One way to do this is to borrow notes from another student—one who takes good notes, that is. Then you can copy the notes and ask questions about information that is not clear to you. When you copy notes, remember to:

► write the main ideas to the left, and put the details underneath, to the right
► try to use the same abbreviations throughout
► leave a space when you miss information so that you can add it later
► do not use complete sentences—these are notes!

ACTIVITY 13 Borrowing notes

Imagine that you were absent from your humanities class. Li, Maria, and Jean Marc are in the same class.

Ask to borrow the lecture notes from the student you think is the best note-taker (See Activity 10).

Copy that student's notes in your notebook.

STRATEGY

Talking about the Lecture

If you can talk about the lecture, it not only helps you understand the material better, but it also shows that you know the material and can probably pass a test. First, use your notes to answer the following questions, and later on, try answering them without looking at your notes.

ACTIVITY 14 Talking about the lecture

Use the notes that you borrowed to answer the following questions about the lecture, "Cry Wolf." (Remember to follow the professor's rules about your roles in the group.)

1. Who was Aesop?

2. What are the four characteristics of Aesop's fables?

3. Tell the fable from the lecture in your own words.

4. What happened at the end of "The Boy Who Cried Wolf"?

5. What's the moral of the story? What situation in your own life could you talk about that illustrates, or serves as an example of, this moral?

6. Look at your notes from Activity 12. What does the professor want the groups to discuss? Can your group do what he wants?

Part 2

 **Looking at Language**

STRATEGY

Word Stress

Pronunciation is important when you speak another language. Often, native speakers of English don't understand non-native speakers because of word stress. In English, putting the stress, or emphasis, on the right syllable of a word is more important than pronouncing individual sounds correctly. When native speakers hear the stress on the wrong syllable, it confuses them, because they expect to hear the stress on a different syllable. In order to be able to use word stress correctly in your speaking, you first have to be able to hear it. *The American Heritage ESL Dictionary*'s definition for a syllable is "a single uninterrupted sound forming a part of a word or in some cases an entire word. The word *house* has one syllable; *houses* has two." All syllables have a vowel sound.

ACTIVITY **15** **Hearing word stress**

Listen to your instructor spell and pronounce these frequently used academic words.

Write the words and then complete the chart.

Compare your answers with a classmate's answers.

You hear: c-r-e-a-t-o-r, *creator*

You write:

Word	Number of syllables	Stressed syllable
creator	3	2

Word	Number of syllables	Stressed syllable
1.		
2.		
3.		
4.		
5.		

▷ Academic Speaking Task 1

Using Your Dictionary for Pronunciation

When you look up a new word in the dictionary, you want to know both the new word's meaning and its pronunciation. Dictionaries use symbols to show you how to pronounce a word. They also separate the word into syllables and show you which syllable is stressed, or pronounced with more emphasis. Because this word stress is more important than the pronunciation of individual sounds, we will use the following method for learning the pronunciation of new words.

Example word: *humanities*

Dictionary: (hyo͞o **măn´** ĭ tēz)

1. Count the number of syllables: 4.
2. Find the stressed syllable: the 2nd.
3. Call *humanities* a 4-2 word.
4. Use some physical movement to show this word stress: tap your fingers, or clap your hands, for example, as you say the word. This helps you remember.

Once you become familiar with this method, you will be able to predict the pronunciation of new words that you read. For example, if you know the word *humanitarian* is a 6-4 word, it will be easier for you to guess the pronunciation.

ACTIVITY 16 **Identifying stress patterns**

Look at these examples from The American Heritage ESL Dictionary.

Pronounce the words after your instructor.

Fill in the chart, and physically make a movement to show the word stress.

Word	Pronunciation	Number of syllables	Stressed syllable	Pattern
lecture	lĕk´chər	2	1	[2-1]
dictation	dĭk tā´shən			[-]
fable	fā´bəl			[-]
synonym	sĭn´ə nĭm´			[-]
universal	yōō´nə vur´səl			[-]

ACTIVITY 17 **Using the dictionary**

Using your own dictionary, fill in the chart and say the word to your partner.

Word	Pronunciation	Number of syllables	Stressed syllable	Pattern
shepherd				[-]
responsible				[-]
philosophical				[-]
individual				[-]
illustrate				[-]

▷ Looking at Language

Be Organized
Master students keep all their class notes and papers organized. They have separate notebooks for different courses, or they use dividers in a three-ring binder. If they need to find something, they know exactly where to look.

POWER GRAMMAR

Question Formation and Pronunciation

Look at the following chart. It gives examples of information questions in English and some common mistakes that ESL students make. Notice the correct use of auxiliaries such as *do, does, is/are, did, can/could,* and *would* to form questions.

When asking questions in English, you need to stress the content words by pronouncing them a little louder than the function words. Remember that the content words (*When, finish*) contain the important ideas in the question. The function words (*does, is, the*) are important for grammar, but not for the information in the question. Notice the stressed syllables in **bold** in the content words in the chart.

Wrong	Right	Verb tense	Information requested
~~What class you take?~~	*What **class**es are you **tak**ing?* ***How** do you **like** your **class**es?*	present progressive simple present	action now, this school term opinion/ preference
~~What time begin class?~~	***What time** does **class** begin?*	simple present	scheduled time
~~When finish this term?~~	***When** does **this term fin**ish?*	simple present	scheduled time (& future event)
~~For when this assignment?~~	***When** is the as**sign**ment **due**?*	simple present	future event
~~Please repeat again about Greece.~~	*Could you **say that** again about **Greece**? or **What** did you **say** about **Greece**?*	past auxiliary simple past	request for repetition
~~Please, give me handout.~~	*Could **I have** a **hand**out? Would **you please give me** a **hand**out? or Do **you have** a**nother hand**out?*	past auxiliary simple present	request for a handout

ACTIVITY **18** **Correcting errors**

Correct the errors in the following questions.

Example: Excuse me, ~~you can~~ help me?
can you

1. What time the library closes?

2. Do you please help me find some information?

3. Where to find this call number?*

4. How much costs the copy machine?

5. You have change for the copy machine?

6. Sorry. What you said?

7. How I check out this book?

8. When this book due?

▷ Academic Speaking Task 2

Asking Questions about English

Sometimes in class, you need to ask questions about the English language. This is especially true in your ESL and English classes. The following questions are frequently used in language classes. You should learn them well so that you can say them automatically, without thinking.

In Order To . . .	Ask This Question . . .
1. ask for a word or phrase in English	*How do you say . . . in English?*
2. ask about the written form of a word	*How do you spell . . . ?*
3. ask about pronunciation	*How do you pronounce . . . ?*
	What's the pronunciation of . . . ?
4. ask about a word's meaning	*What does . . . mean?*
	What's the meaning of . . . ?

call number = the numbers and letters on a book that tell you where it is in the library

5. ask about differences between the meanings of two words

6. ask about a word you heard but don't remember now

7. ask for repetition

What's the difference between ...and...?
What word did you use for...?

I'm sorry. Could you please repeat that? Excuse me?
(with rising intonation and a questioning look on your face)

ACTIVITY 19   **Asking questions about language**

Listen to the situations on page 228 (see Appendix 1) and decide which question to ask. Do the first three and then switch.

Example:

Student A (on page 228): *You know how to say the word "unique," but you don't know how to write it.*

Student B (book closed): *How do you spell "unique"?*

▷ Looking at Language and Culture

Academic Culture: Participating in Class

As a college student, you are expected to attend class and speak up when the instructor asks a question. This is true for questions about the course material and for questions about your opinions and personal experience. Most instructors encourage their students to speak up and share their opinions, even when they disagree with something. Class participation is important! When a college professor asks a question, he or she expects an answer almost immediately. If there is no response in three or four seconds, the professor thinks the students don't know the answer. This means that you have little time to plan an answer—you need to respond quickly.

Nonverbal communication: taking turns in discussions

Nonverbal communication, or body language, is often more important than spoken language when you want to participate in class. In large classes, if you want to speak, you should raise your hand (but sometimes students just call out their questions or comments) to attract the instructor's attention. In small-group discussions, you also need to physically show that you want to say something, or want a turn speaking. First, you need to use eye contact—you have to be looking directly at the person who is speaking or at the discussion leader. You can also do the following:

- ▶ nod or shake your head
- ▶ hold up your index finger
- ▶ sit forward in your chair

STRATEGY

Phrases for Interrupting

In addition to using body language, you need to say something to show that you would like to speak. If it's a lively discussion, you may have to try several times. Here is a list of introductory phrases you can use:

Excuse me, . . .	*In my opinion, . . .*
That's right, but . . .	*I think . . .*
I agree, but . . .	*I don't think . . .*
Yes, but . . .	*I disagree . . .*
That may be true, but . . .	*Don't you think . . . ?*
Well, . . .	*Do you really think . . .*

ACTIVITY 20 **Role-playing**

Take turns playing the role of the person who interrupts while the rest of the group talks about the pictures that follow.

What is this person "saying"?

▷ Academic Speaking Task 3

Participating in Discussions

It is important to participate in class discussions for two reasons. First, it helps you learn the material in the class, because the ideas will be more clear if you verbalize, or talk about them. Second, it lets the instructor know that you are alive, awake, and aware of what's happening in the class. You will leave a positive impression on the instructor if you are an active participant in class discussions.

In the humanities class in this chapter, the professor has given the students instructions, or rules, for a small-group discussion. Even though the rules help control the behavior of the group, discussions often seem chaotic, or unorganized, because two or three people speak at the same time, they interrupt each other, and sometimes they appear rude. This is OK (except for the rudeness); it's a natural part of classroom discussions. It would be nice if everyone in the group let one person speak and listened politely until that person finished, but that rarely happens in a typical class.

Look at the following scale, or continuum, which measures the behavior of people participating in group discussions, and notice that in this culture, both ends of the continuum are negative. Positive behavior is somewhere in the middle. People don't always agree on what behavior they consider positive or negative, so you have to be careful with behavior that might be offensive to some.

☹ Passive	☺ Assertive	☹ Aggressive
▸ quiet	▸ polite	▸ loud and rude
▸ avoids direct eye contact	▸ looks at people directly	▸ always interrupts
▸ never speaks	▸ listens to others	▸ doesn't listen to others
	▸ expresses opinions	
	▸ comfortable disagreeing with others	
	▸ respects others' opinions	

ACTIVITY 21 Talking about talking

Answer these questions, following the humanities professor's instructions for small-group discussions.

1. When you worked in a small group earlier in this chapter, who was the best participant? Why?
2. On the scale above, if the extreme left is 0, the middle is 5, and the extreme right is 10, what number are you? Why?
3. Would you like to be a lower or a higher number? Explain.
4. What can you do to become a better participant in class discussions?

STRATEGY

Applying What You've Learned

In college, professors expect students to apply what they've studied to new situations and/or to their own lives. This shows that the students have learned the material, not just memorized it. Memorize means to put in your memory, but it has the additional negative idea that you don't understand the material.

ACTIVITY 22 Applying what you've learned

Read the following fable, "A Wolf in Sheep's Clothing," and answer the questions.

One day a shepherd was watching his sheep. There was a wolf nearby, and he wanted to get closer to the sheep, but the shepherd and his sheep dog were watching too closely.

Then the wolf saw the skin of a dead sheep, and he used it to cover himself. When it got dark, he hid under the sheep-skin and joined the flock. The shepherd didn't see the wolf until it was too late.

The moral of the story: Beware of a wolf in sheep's clothing.

1. Without looking at your lecture notes, can you explain how this fable has or doesn't have the characteristics of a fable given in the lecture?
2. Can you give an example from your own life of someone who cried wolf? How about someone who was a wolf in sheep's clothing?

Part 3

ASSESSING YOUR LISTENING AND SPEAKING SKILLS

▷ Getting Ready for the Test: Self-Assessment

ACTIVITY 23 **Evaluating your skills**

Evaluate yourself on the following skills by putting a (✓) in the column that best describes how you feel you can do each. For every check in the third column, go back and practice before you take the test.

Listening I am able to:	Great	OK	Need to practice
1. take notes while listening to a lecture			
2. use my notes to answer questions about the information			
3. listen to new words & identify the stressed syllable			
4. listen for definitions of words			
5. understand & use new vocabulary			

Speaking I can:	Great	OK	Need to practice
1. find, name, & talk about countries on a map			
2. tell an Aesop's fable in my own words			
3. use my notes to discuss a lecture & answer questions			
4. use a dictionary to pronounce a new word with correct stress & identify the number of syllables			
5. ask questions about English words: meaning, pronunciation, & spelling			
6. participate in class discussions using verbal & nonverbal communication			
Study skills I should:			
1. be familiar with vocabulary before listening to a lecture			
2. recognize good lecture notes			
3. try to pay attention & be organized			
4. borrow notes from a classmate when I miss a class			
5. apply what I've studied to new situations			

▽ Chapter Test

To evaluate your progress, your instructor may ask you to do some or all of the following activities for the chapter test.

Listening Test Activities

ACTIVITY 24 **Listening for definitions**

Listen to the following sentences. In the first column, write the word that the professor defines. In the second column, write the definition.

Word	Definition
1.	
2.	
3.	
4.	

ACTIVITY 25 Listening for word stress

Listen to the words and fill in the chart.

You hear: villagers

Word	Number of syllables	Stressed syllable	Pattern
Example: *villagers*	3	1	[3–1]
1.			
2.			
3.			
4.			
5.			
6.			

ACTIVITY 26   Using your dictionary for pronunciation

Listen to your instructor spell the following words. Write the words. Then, using your dictionary, find the pronunciation and stress.

	Word	Pronunciation	Number of syllables	Stressed syllable	Pattern
1.					
2.					
3.					
4.					
5.					

Speaking Test Activities

ACTIVITY 27 **Answering questions about the lecture**

Answer the questions you hear about the lecture "Cry Wolf." (Your instructor may ask you to answer them orally or in writing.)

1.

2.

3.

4.

5.

ACTIVITY 28 **Talking about Aesop's fables**

Listen to your instructor and answer one question about a fable from the chapter.

ACTIVITY 29 **Asking questions about language**

Listen to your instructor and ask the appropriate question.

Speaking Evaluation Checklist

Your instructor may use the following checklist to assess your speaking in class activities and/or in the Speaking Test.

Speaking evaluation	OK	Needs work	Example(s)
Listening			
► understood question			
Content			
► answered correctly			
Language use			
► expressed ideas clearly			
► used language from chapter			
Pronunciation			
► clear & comprehensible			
► not too fast or slow			
► loud enough			
Nonverbal communication			
► appropriate eye contact			
► correct posture			

WEB POWER
You will find additional exercises related to the content in this chapter at http://esl.college.hmco.com/students.

Food Chains

ACADEMIC FOCUS: NATURAL SCIENCE ▶ ECOLOGY

Academic Listening and Speaking Objectives

In this chapter, you will work individually, in pairs, and in small groups to:

- ▶ Learn about land biomes and food chains
- ▶ Use abbreviations and mathematical symbols in your notes
- ▶ Understand and use cardinal and ordinal numbers
- ▶ Put your notes in outline form and compare notes with a classmate
- ▶ Address people correctly in formal and informal situations
- ▶ Talk on the telephone and leave a message
- ▶ Talk about charts and graphs
- ▶ Predict test questions

Part 1

EFFECTIVE ACADEMIC LISTENING

The lecture in this chapter, "Food Chains," comes from a natural science course. Natural sciences, such as biology, deal with nature and the physical world. To get ready for the lecture on food chains, you need to understand certain terms, or words. One of these terms is *biome*. Land biomes are large areas that have similar climates, or weather, and certain plants and animals. There are six major land biomes in the world: tundra, coniferous forest, deciduous forest, grassland, desert, and rainforest.

▷ Getting Ready for the Lecture

ACTIVITY 1 Identifying land biomes

To get ready for this chapter's lecture, look at the following illustrations and label each of the six major land biomes. Use #1 as an example. (Remember to use the roles you learned in Chapter 1, page 14.)

1. tundra

2. _____

3. _____

4. _____

5. _____

6. _____

Hints for Completing Activity 1

   2. Brazil is famous for this type of biome.

   3. Another name for this biome is *savannah*.

   4. The trees in this biome are evergreens, which means they are green all year round.

   5. This biome exists on almost all continents, e.g., the Sahara in Africa.

   6. In the autumn, the leaves on the trees in this biome change from green to bright orange, red, and yellow, before falling to the ground.

ACTIVITY 2 **Talking about biomes**

Follow the Chapter 1 guidelines about group discussions, and answer these questions. Change roles in the group: if you were a group member before, you should be the leader, the note-taker, or the timekeeper now.

1. Using the words from the list, fill in the chart with the name of one plant and one animal that live there. The first one is done for you as an example.

cactus   moose   pine tree*

camel   moss   polar bear

grass*   oak tree   squirrel*

monkey   palm tree   zebra

BIOME	tundra	coniferous forest	deciduous forest	grassland	desert	rainforest
PLANT	moss					
ANIMAL						

2. What biome do you live in?
3. What biomes are these cities in? (Use the map from Chapter 1 to help you.)

   Cairo, Egypt

   Quebec, Canada

   Bangkok, Thailand

   Rio de Janeiro, Brazil

   Fairbanks, Alaska

*This lives in two biomes, but it is more common in one.

Note-taking: Using Abbreviations and Symbols

As you studied in Chapter 1, notes are used for remembering information. When you take notes during a lecture, you should write the important ideas. It is difficult to take notes, however, when professors speak fast. That's why you need to use abbreviations and symbols in your notes.

Some abbreviations are the beginning of words, and some come from Latin. Many symbols are from mathematics. Look at these examples:

Word/Idea You Hear	Abbreviation/Symbol You Write
professor	prof
chapter	ch or chap
information	info

Try completing the list of examples with these symbols and abbreviations:

in. or "   cm   e.g.   =   +   ft. or '

for example, an example of this

is/are, means, is the same as, equals . . .

plus, and, in addition, positive . . .

centimeter(s)

inches

feet

ACTIVITY 3 Understanding abbreviations and math symbols

Match the idea with the correct abbreviation or symbol on the right. Look at #1 as an example.

1. ____>____ more than, greater than, is made up of   ≈

2. _____ a lot more than, many more than, much greater than   %

3. _____ less than, fewer than, is part of   ×

4. _____ different   grp

5. _____ a lot less than, much less than, many fewer than   ∴

6. _____ plus or minus, give or take   >>

7. _____ group   thru

8. _____ percent, percentage   <<

9. _____ approximately, around, more or less   ±

10. _____ government   diff.

11. _____ multiplied by, times   ≠

12. _____ number (and "pound")   #

13. _____ therefore, so, thus, consequently   <

14. _____ not the same as, not equal to   >

15. _____ through   govt

STRATEGY

Listening for Numbers

Professors use numbers in lectures to organize information (*There are three reasons for . . . We classify these into four major groups . . .*) and to support statements with facts (*Scientists estimate there are 111 million species on earth*). You need to understand these numbers and include them in your notes.

Cardinal numbers (*one, two, three . . .*) are used to indicate how many things there are, whereas ordinal numbers (*first, second, third . . .*) are used to show the order of things. You can write ordinal numbers two ways: *first* or *1st, second* or *2nd, third* or *3rd*. See Appendix 2 for a complete list.

ACTIVITY **4** **Listening for numbers**

Listen to the following sentences and fill in the space with the correct number. (Be careful—at least one is written with letters, not numbers.) Look at #1 as an example.

1. In ___1804___ , Captain Meriwether Lewis and Captain William Clark were

    sent by U.S. President Thomas Jefferson to explore the American West.

2. They kept journals and described what they saw: _____ animals and

    _____ plants.

3. At the time of Lewis and Clark, there were _____ grizzly bears in the

    West. Now there are fewer than _____ in Idaho, Wyoming, and

    Montana.

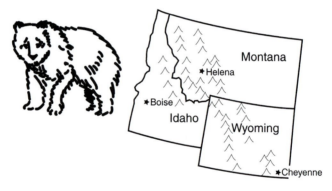

4. On September _____ in South Dakota, Lewis wrote in his journal

    that he could see a herd of buffalo, or bison, with as many as _____

    animals.

5. _____ years ago there were as many as _____

    bison, but only a few _____ were living at the beginning of the

    _____ century.

6. There were almost _____ prairie dogs at the time of Lewis

and Clark, but the population has decreased by more than _____.

Source: From "Lewis & Clark's America," pp. 42–46, *Sierra*, May/June 2002,
Vol. 87, No. 3. by Todd Wilkinson and Paul Rauber.

POWER GRAMMAR

That Is (i.e.)

It is often necessary for speakers or writers to try to explain themselves
by repeating their ideas using different words. (You saw this in Chapter 1
with the use of *or*.) When doing this, they can warn the reader or listener
beforehand by saying:

in other words	*meaning*
that is	*I mean*
that is to say	*what I mean is*
i.e. (from Latin, *id est*, used more in writing	
than speaking)	

Example: *Bacteria, in other words, very small one-celled
organisms, are decomposers.*

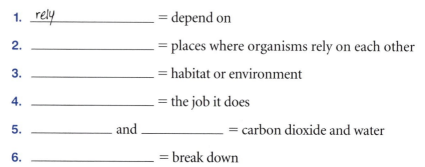

ACTIVITY 5   Listening for explanations

Listen to the following, and write the word or phrase that the professor explains in the ecology lecture. Look at #1 as an example.

1. _rely_____ = depend on

2. _____ = places where organisms rely on each other

3. _____ = habitat or environment

4. _____ = the job it does

5. _____ and _____ = carbon dioxide and water

6. _____ = break down

S T R A T E G Y

Words from the Lecture

In every class, you are expected to understand and use certain words that are important in that subject. The professor in the science lecture uses the following words. In addition, he or she explains a lot of new terms that are not included here.

aquarium	Great Plains
biome	interact
branch	make up
chain	organism
classify	pond
concept	savannah
cycle	snake
environment	species

ACTIVITY 6 **Expanding your vocabulary**

Match the words on page 44 with the definitions that follow. Then check your answers by listening to your instructor. Look at #1 as an example.

1. _concept_ An idea.

2. _____ To act on each other.

3. _____ All of the surroundings and conditions, such as water, air, and soil, that affect living things.

4. _____ A part or division of a larger whole.

5. _____ A living thing.

6. _____ A small lake.

7. _____ A glass tank filled with water used for displaying fish.

8. _____ Elevated plains region in the U.S. and Canada, east of the Rocky Mountains.

9. _____ A large area that has the same climate and organisms.

10. _____ To form, constitute.

11. _____ A group of plants or animals that are considered the same kind and that can breed naturally and produce offspring.

12. _____ To put into categories or classes; categorize.

13. _____ A series of events that is periodically repeated.

14 _____ A series of connected or related things.

15. _____ A reptile with a long, narrow body and no legs. Some are poisonous.

ACTIVITY 7 **Practicing word stress**

Choose a word and say it aloud.

Listen to your partner say the stress pattern that he or she hears.

Tell your partner if the stress pattern is right or not.

Do the odd or even numbers, and then switch.

Remember to tap out the syllables with your fingers or use some other physical movement to feel the syllables and stress.

Example:

[2-2]	[3-2]
assess assessed	assesses assessment

Student A: *Assessed.*
Student B: *2-2.*
Student A: *Right.*

1.

[3-1]	[4-1]
consequent consequence	consequences consequently

2.

[2-1]	[3-1]
process processed	processes processing

3.

[2-2]	[3-2]	[4-2]
percent	percentage	percentages

4.

[2-2]	[3-2]	[4-3]
define defined	defining	definition definitions

5.

[4-2]	[5-4]	[6-4]
environment	environmental	environmentalist environmentally

6.

[2-1]	[4-2]	[5-2]	[6-2]
concept	conceptual	conceptualize conceptualized	conceptualizes

7.

[3-1]	[4-3]	[5-3]
energy	energetic	energetically

8.

[4-2]	[5-2]	[6-4]	[6-5]
identify identified identity	identifying	identifiable	identification

ACTIVITY 8   Using academic words

With a partner, practice asking and answering the questions on page 229 (see Appendix 1). Ask the first four questions, while your partner scans the words in Activity 7 for the answers. Then switch roles.

Example:

Student A (reading from page 229): *What do you call a person who cares about the environment?*

Student B (looking at pages 46–47): *An environmentalist.*

▷ Getting Information from the Lecture

Note-taking: Identifying Important Terms

In Chapter 1, you learned that lecturers stress important words and that good notes should include those keywords and main ideas. The chapter's lecture includes many new words, with definitions, and important ideas. The professor stresses this vocabulary in the lecture because it's important in the field of natural science. It's important for you to know because it will be on the test.

ACTIVITY 9   Looking at notes

Look at the lecture notes in Activity 10, and answer these questions.

1. The notes in Activity 10 are in outline form. What is an outline?
2. What abbreviations are used in the notes? What do they mean?
3. What symbols are used? What do they mean?
4. Try "reading" the notes aloud, i.e., translate from note form to complete sentences.

ACTIVITY 10 Listening for important terms

The following lecture notes are in outline form, but the important terms are missing.

1. *Listen to the lecture and fill in the words that the professor explains.*
2. *Don't worry about the correct spelling—your instructor will spell the words for you later.*
3. *Use the first one as an example.*

• Ecology > <u>ecosystems</u> > food chains + webs

   ▪ defin. of _____ = grp of parts that wrk together

      ▲ ex.: politics, gov't, & anatomy

   ▪ biology: _____ : where organisms + environ.

   rely on each other, i.e., interdpndt elements = plants
   + animals + environt., can be small, like pond, or lrge, like desert

• Great Plains ecosyst. < grassland or savannah biome

   ▪ 3 characʼstics of savannah:

     1. abund. of _____
     2. hot summers
     3. enough rain so not desert, but not enough for forests

   ▪ each species has _____ & _____

      ▲ _____ = place plant/animal lives in ecosys.,

      e.g., buffalo on plains, gopher undrgrnd

      ▲ _____ = job it does, eg bison eats grass +

      moves, flowers use sun to make food thru . . .

      ▲ _____ = chemical process plants w chlorophyll

      use sun to make food frm CO_2 + H_2O

   ▪ transfer of matter + energy as plants + animals interact

      ▲ ecosyst. > food chains + interconnected f.chains = fd web

■ food chain in grassland ecosyst.

 ▲ 3 types of organisms in ecosys:

 I. _____: make own food, e.g., grass, clover, dandelions, wildflowers

 2. _____: eats other organisms

 ◆ diff. levels, depndng on position: Ist order, 2nd, etc.

 ◆ ex. of grasshopper, eats grass, so Ist order cons.

 ◆ prairie dog eats grass + grsshoppers so Ist order cons. in I chain, but 2nd in other

 ◆ hawks + snakes eat p. dogs, so 3rd order

 ◆ bison eat grass, so Ist ord.

 3. _____: break down dead orgs so can be used by producers; ex. = bacteria + fungi (mushrms)

ACTIVITY 11 **Note-taking**

Close the book, listen to the last part of the lecture again, and take notes in your notebook. Remember to use abbreviations and mathematical symbols. Try organizing the ideas in outline form.

◹ Recognizing Teacher Talk

The important vocabulary that professors explain in their lectures is found in the textbook. Other terms that you are expected to know will **not** necessarily be in the book, so if you don't know them, you need to write them in your notes. To indicate these terms, professors might say:

"Remember that . . ."
"You will recall . . ."
"You know that . . ."
"You should know that . . ."

ACTIVITY 12 **Recognizing teacher talk**

Listen to excerpts of the lecture, and write what the professor expects you to know. If you need to, write the explanations, too.

1.

2.

▷ Using Your Lecture Notes

Study Strategy: Comparing Notes

One way to make sure you understood a lecture is to compare notes with a classmate. Sometimes your classmate will have information that you don't have in your notes, and sometimes you'll have information that your partner needs. By talking to each other about the lecture, you will understand and remember more of the information.

ACTIVITY **13** **Comparing notes**

Sit facing your partner, and take turns using your notes to "lecture" to each other about food chains.

Talk for two minutes, and then listen to your partner continue from where you ended.

Continue with two-minute turns until you have finished the lecture.

Part 2

EFFECTIVE ACADEMIC SPEAKING

▷ Academic Speaking Task 1

Speaking to Learn

In order to learn new information in your college classes, you need to do a lot: read your textbooks, go to class, listen attentively, take notes, and study outside of class. How do you know that you have learned the material and are ready for a test? One way to know is by speaking. As explained in Chapter 1, if you can speak about the material without looking at your notes, you should feel confident that you have learned it. Talking about the material includes summarizing the information in your own words, explaining the new words, and applying the concepts to new situations. If you can't speak about the subject, then you need to spend more time studying.

ACTIVITY 14   **Speaking to learn**

Study your lecture notes from "Food Chains." Then look at the illustration of this food web. Using the vocabulary from the lecture ("producer, consumer," etc.), identify the organisms in this food web and discuss the relationships among them with your group.

▷ Looking at Language

STRATEGY

Using Cardinal and Ordinal Numbers

It is important to be familiar with cardinal and ordinal numbers because they are frequently used in academic lectures. College professors use numbers in examples to support their main ideas. For instance, history professors mention a lot of dates and other time expressions. Economics and sociology professors include a lot of numbers, especially percentages, ranges, and amounts. Numbers should be included in your lecture notes for all subjects—not just mathematics and statistics.

Pronunciation: Thought Groups

Thought groups are words that English speakers pronounce together as a meaningful group. At the end of a thought group, they pause and lower the tone (*do, ti, la, so, fa, mi, re, do*) of their voice. The lower tone tells the listener that it's the end of the thought, or idea, and the pause gives the listener time to process the information. Thought groups are especially important in the pronunciation of numbers because they indicate which numbers go together. Look at the following example of a telephone number:

(920)	733	-0435	or 920.733.0435
↑	↑	↑	
area code	exchange	number	
(Group 1)	(Group 2)	(Group 3)	

When you say the entire phone number, you pause (indicated by a comma) and lower the tone of your voice at the end of each group: *nine two zero, seven three three, oh four three five.*

In the following chart, pronunciation is indicated two ways. The end of each thought group has a comma (,), and the syllable that is stressed the most in the phrase is in **bold** print.

When You See:		You Say:
Centuries:	the 20th c.	*the **twen**tieth **cen**tury*
Years:	the 1960s	*the nineteen **six**ties*
	1964	*nineteen sixty-**four***
	AD 2005	*AD (anno Domini) two thousand **five***
	2010	*two thousand **ten**, OR twenty **ten***
	502 BC	*five oh two BC OR five hundred two BC (before Christ)*

(Continued)

When You See:		You Say:
Dates:	Nov. 22, 1963 11-22-63 OR 11/22/63	*November twenty-second, nineteen sixty-three*
	June 6, 1944	*June sixth, nineteen forty-four*
Times:	8:00 a.m.	*eight o'clock a.m. OR eight o'clock in the morning*
	8:10	*eight ten, ten after eight, OR ten past eight*
	8:30 p.m.	*eight thirty p.m. OR half past eight in the evening*
	8:45	*eight forty-five OR quarter to nine*
	8:50	*eight fifty OR ten to nine*
	3:20 p.m.	*three twenty p.m. OR twenty after three in the afternoon*
Addresses:	5280 NW 33rd St.	*fifty-two eighty, northwest thirty- third street*
Zip codes:	54914	*five four nine one four*
Phone numbers:	(212) 749-1580	*area code, two one two, seven four nine, one five eight oh/zero OR area code, two one two, seven four nine, fifteen eighty*
Percentages:	73%	*seventy-three percent*
Amounts:*	5280'	*five thousand, two hundred, (and) eighty feet*
	12"	*twelve inches*
	58 cm	*fifty-eight centimeters*
Ranges:	75–80%	*between seventy-five and eighty percent* *OR from seventy-five, to eighty percent*
Prices:	$15.99	*fifteen dollars, and ninety-nine cents, or fifteen ninety-nine*
	$1599.00	*one thousand, five hundred, (and) ninety-nine dollars, OR fifteen ninety-nine*

*When exact numbers are not known, people often use expressions such as
dozens of, hundreds of, thousands of, millions of . . . For example, *Hundreds of
insects live in an anthill.*

ACTIVITY **15**   **Reading numbers**

Work with a partner to read the following numbers. Do the odd or even numbers, and then switch.

1. $17.95 (2 ways)
2. 5:45 a.m. (2 ways)
3. 356,000
4. 25–35%
5. April 2, 2003
6. 600 BC
7. (915) 572-4627
8. 7220 SE 8th St.
9. 3:15 p.m. (2 ways)
10. the 15th cent.

◢ Academic Speaking Task 2

Describing Graphs and Charts

Both professors and textbooks use different kinds of charts and graphs to show information visually. A pie chart is circular, in the shape of a pie or pizza. A bar graph has an x and y axis: the x axis is horizontal, meaning it goes side to side, or left to right, and the y axis is vertical, meaning it goes from bottom to top. The length of the bar represents a number; the higher the number, the longer the bar.

When describing a graph or chart, you should start with the title to give a general idea of what information it shows. Then explain what the graph is comparing and what the numbers represent (percentages, number of inches, dollars . . .). Mention any big differences that you see and what those differences might mean. Listen to the example below.

This bar graph/pie chart shows the number of native bird species in four countries: Brazil, Indonesia, Ecuador, and the United States. Brazil, Indonesia, and Ecuador have the highest number of species. Brazil has one thousand five hundred seventy-three, Indonesia has one thousand five hundred nineteen, and Ecuador has one thousand four hundred thirty-five native bird species. The United States has the lowest number with three hundred forty-six. Even though the United States is the largest of the four countries, it has a lot fewer native bird species. Maybe this is because it is the most developed of the four countries, and development might mean destruction of the birds' habitats.

Number of Native Bird Species

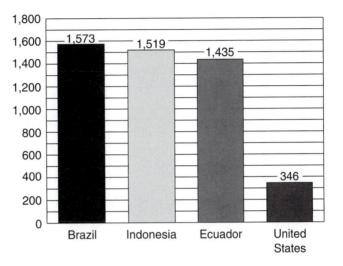

Number of Native Bird Species

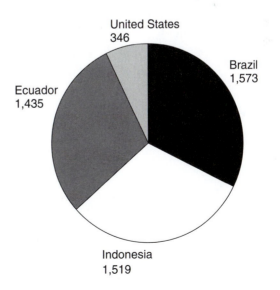

ACTIVITY 16   **Describing graphs and charts**

Answer the following questions orally:

The Earth's Biomes

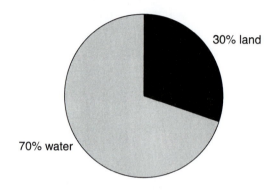

30% land

70% water

1. How much of the earth's surface do oceans, seas, rivers, and lakes cover?
2. Which of the following opinions might use this chart as support? Why?
   a. We need to do more research on marine, or water, biomes.
   b. Soon we will not have enough water on Earth.

The Earth's Water

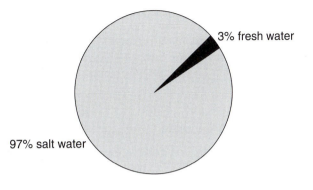

3. How much of the water on Earth is fresh, and how much is saltwater?
4. Which of the following opinions might use this chart as support? Why?
   a. We need to learn how to purify saltwater to use for drinking.
   b. Soon we will not have enough water on Earth.

Average Annual Rainfall

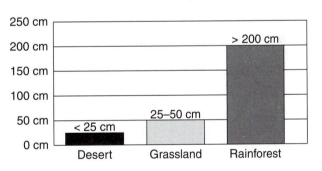

5. How much rain do grasslands receive annually?
6. What is the average annual rainfall in the desert biome?
7. On average, how much rain does the rainforest biome receive per year?
8. Where do you think most of the world's species live? Why?
9. Describe each chart, explaining the information it shows.

▷ Looking at Language and Culture

Formal vs. Informal Language: Addressing People Correctly

In all cultures, people speak differently to others, depending on their relationship, ages, and social situation. One way to show these differences is in the way you address someone, that is, what you call that person when you're speaking to her or him. The following descriptions are general; you will find a lot of individual differences among people. Treat people with respect no matter who they are—or seem to be. If you're not sure how to address someone, begin at the formal level. If the person feels uncomfortable, she or he will tell you, "Please call me _____."

Formal language: used with people in authority, e.g., your academic advisor, instructor, supervisor/boss at work, a judge, or a police officer, in structured situations, e.g., a meeting, courtroom, or parent/instructor consultation.

Informal language: used with your peers, i.e., people who are at the same level as you, for example your classmates, coworkers, or friends.

Intimate language: used with people who are very close to you: your husband/wife, boyfriend/girlfriend, and best friends.

Rude language: used with people you are angry with and want to insult, or offend—not recommended! Be careful—by using language or a gesture,* you can offend people and not be aware of it.

The following chart is a guide for some forms of address; if you know any others, share them with the class, and add them to the chart.

*gesture = hand or body movement used to communicate

Names and titles:	Kim O'Malley, MD Donna Martinez, Adjunct Professor Michelle Curtis, PhD Katie Smith-Watson Diana Jones, elementary-school instructor (single)	Corey Mass, judge Steve Hansen, police officer Tom Woo, Pres. & CEO Kevin Nash

To address	Formal	Informal	Intimate	Rude

A person whose name you know	A male: *Mr. Woo*
	A female: *Ms. Jones* or
	    Miss Jones
	    Ms. Smith-Watson or
	    Mrs. Smith-Watson
	M or F: *Doctor O' Malley*
	    Professor Martinez
	    Dr. Curtis
	    Judge Mass
	    Officer Hansen
		Kim,
		Steve …
		(person's first name)
			Honey
			Sweetheart
			Sweetie
			Dear
				Honey
				Sweetheart
				Sweetie
				Dearie
				(if you don't know the person well and it's a formal situation)

A person whose profession you know, but not the name	College instructor: *Professor* MD or PhD: *Doctor* Police: *Officer* Judge: *Your Honor*	N/A	N/A	Anything other than *Ma'am, Sir,* or the correct form for the person's profession.
Two or more people (you don't know their names)	Females: *Ladies* Males: *Gentlemen* M and Fs: *Ladies and gentlemen*	M and Fs: *(You) guys.*	N/A	M and Fs: *(You) guys*
One person (you don't know her/his name)	A female: *Miss, Ma'am* A male: *Sir*	N/A	N/A	A female: *Lady*
To get a person's attention	*Excuse me.*	*Excuse me.* *Hey.*	*Honey* *Sweetheart* *Sweetie*	*Hey.* *Hey, you*

N/A = Not Applicable (Not possible)

ACTIVITY 17 **Addressing people correctly**

Read the following descriptions and decide with your partner how you would address the people in each situation. Use the forms of address in the chart above. Feel free to add your own.

1. Donna Martinez, Adjunct Professor (She is your neighbor.)
   a. You take a class at the local college, and she is the professor. You see her going to work in the morning. What do you call her?
   b. You see her in class in the evening. How do you address her?

2. Kevin Nash, office worker
   You need to apply for financial aid. Kevin Nash works in the financial aid office and is behind the counter when you arrive. What do you say to him?

3. Michelle Curtis, PhD
   Michelle Curtis is your instructor for Ecology 1101. You are having trouble understanding the chapter on biomes and food chains, so you go to see her during her office hours. How do you begin the conversation?

4. You're at the school library and need some help. One of the librarians, a young woman, is sitting at a desk reading a book. What do you say?

5. You're driving on the highway, and a state trooper*stops you, and asks to see your driver's license. Then he or she asks, "Do you know how fast you were driving?" How do you answer?

state trooper = a state highway police officer

P O W E R   G R A M M A R

This Is vs. *I Am*

This, singular, and *these,* plural, are used for things and people close to the speaker. *This* is also used on the telephone and in introductions. On the phone, one way to ask the name of the person you're speaking to is, *Who's this?* You also say *This is . . .* for giving your own name. In person, however, use *this* only when you are introducing someone else. Say "I am" when giving your name in person and on the computer (e-mails and chatrooms).

In Person	On the Telephone
Example 1: **A:** *Who are you?**	**A:** *Who is this, please?* or *Who's speaking, please?*
B: *I'm Kathy.*	**B:** *This is Kathy.*
Example 2: **A:** *Are you Kathy?*	**A:** *Is this Kathy?*
B: *Yes, I'm Kathy.*	**B:** *Yes, this is Kathy.*

Introductions

Example 3: **A:** *Joan, this is my friend, John.*
      John, this is my sister, Joan.
   B: *Hi, John.*
   C: *Nice to meet you, Joan.*

Example 4: **A:** *Hi, I'm Emily.*
   B: *Hi, Emily. I'm Tom.*
      Nice to meet you.
   A: *Nice to meet you, too.*

*considered rude by most people

STRATEGY

Intonation

Intonation, or change in tone (*do, re, mi, fa, so, la, ti, do*), is what makes a language sound like music. In English, intonation is important when asking questions, because your voice should go up or down, depending on the type of question. When you ask a yes/no question, your voice should go **up** at the end, but when you ask an information question (*who, what, why . . .*), your voice should go **down**. Listen to the rising and falling intonation as your instructor and two classmates read the telephone conversations below. The arrows indicate the correct intonation.

🎧 Ring, ring . . .

    A: *Hello?* ↗

    B: *Hello, is this Kathy?* ↗

    A: *No, it isn't.* ↘ *I think you have the wrong number.* ↘
        What number are you calling? ↘

    B: *Is this 645-8682?* ↗

    A: *No, it isn't.* ↘

    B: *Oh, sorry.* ↘

🎧 Ring, ring . . .

    C: *Hello?* ↗

    B: *Hello, is Kathy there, please?* ↗

    C: *This is Kathy.* ↘

    B: *Hi, Kathy.* ↘ *This is Julie.* ↘

ACTIVITY 18 **Making a telephone call**

Work with a partner to write a short telephone conversation. Then read your conversation to the rest of the class, using the correct intonation.

▽ Academic Speaking Task 3

Talking on the Telephone

When making a telephone call to get information or make an appointment, you don't have to give your name if the person answering the phone doesn't know you. Just say "hello," and ask your question or say why you are calling. If the person knows you, however, identify yourself by saying, "This is . . ." before giving the reason you're calling.

Example 1: **A:** *Hello, Jefferson College Library. How may I help you?*

B: *Hello. Can you tell me your hours, please?*

Example 2: **A:** *Hello, Dr. Jackson speaking.*

B: *Dr. Jackson, this is _____. I'm in your 1100 class. I'm calling to make an appointment. I need to talk to you about the last quiz.*

Leaving a message

When leaving a phone message, you need to identify yourself, say why you're calling, and leave your number so that the person can call you back. Speak slowly and clearly so that the person has enough time to write down the information, and repeat your number. For example,

Hello, Professor Bahamonde. This is Jean-Paul Bonamie from your ecology class. I'm calling to ask a question about the homework. Could you please call me back at 347-3175? That's 347-3175. I'll be here until 6:00 tonight, Thursday. Thank you.

ACTIVITY 19 Role-playing by telephone

Work with a partner to play these roles on the telephone. Remember to address each person correctly.

1. Call the computer lab at school to find out their hours.
2. Call your instructor to make an appointment.
3. Call the bookstore to ask if they have a particular textbook.
4. Call your classmate to ask for help with the homework. Leave a message.
5. You were absent from class. Call a classmate to find out what you missed.

STRATEGY

Predicting Test Questions

Whenever you have a test, you need to decide what to study, in other words, what you think the professor expects you to know. How do you know what to study? The information is important if the professor:

▶ tells you it's going to be on the test
▶ talks about it in class, and it's in the textbook, too
▶ writes it on the board

Master Student Tip

▼ **Get Ready for the Lecture**

Most professors lecture about the same material as the textbook, so it is to your advantage, or benefit, to read the chapter before you hear the lecture, especially with a topic like natural science. There are many new, specialized words, and you will become familiar with that vocabulary by reading the chapter before you hear the lecture.

ACTIVITY 20 Predicting test questions

Work with a group to study for a test.

Think about questions a natural science professor might ask about food chains, and write them here.

a. _____

b. _____

c. _____

d. _____

e. _____

See if other groups can answer your questions.

Part 3

ASSESSING YOUR LISTENING AND SPEAKING SKILLS

▷ Getting Ready for the Test: Self-Assessment

ACTIVITY 21 Evaluating your skills

Evaluate yourself on the following skills by putting a check mark in the column that best describes how you feel you can do each. For every check mark in the third column, go back and practice before you take the test.

Listening I can:	Great	OK	Need to practice
1. use abbreviations & mathematical symbols in my notes			
2. understand cardinal & ordinal numbers (*two, second*)			
3. understand expressions used for repetition/explanation (*i.e., that is, in other words*)			
4. recognize important words in a lecture			
5. understand & use academic words			
Speaking I am able to:			
1. talk about biomes, food chains, & webs			
2. pronounce a word when given the number of syllables & stress, e.g., [*3-1*]			

Speaking (cont.) I am able to:	Great	OK	Need to practice
3. read cardinal & ordinal numbers aloud (in dates, percentages, etc.)			
4. explain the information given in a chart or graph			
5. address people correctly in different social situations			
6. talk on the telephone & leave a message			
Study skills I should:			
1. listen to a science lecture & take notes			
2. put notes in outline form			
3. compare notes with a classmate's			
4. focus on my long-term goals			
5. get ready for the lecture			
6. apply what I've studied to new situations			
7. predict test questions			

▽ Chapter Test

In order to evaluate your progress, your instructor may ask you to do some or all of the following activities for the chapter test.

Listening Test Activities

ACTIVITY 22   **Using numbers, symbols, and abbreviations**

Listen to the following phrases and take notes. Remember to write numbers, symbols, and abbreviations.

1.

2.

3.

4.

5.

ACTIVITY 23   **Using math abbreviations and symbols**

Listen to the following sentences and take notes. Remember to use abbreviations and mathematical symbols.

1.

2.

3.

4.

5.

ACTIVITY 24   **Answering questions about the lecture**

Answer the questions you hear about the lecture, "Food Chains." (Your instructor may ask you to answer them orally or in writing.)

1.

2.

3.

Speaking Test Activities

ACTIVITY 25 **Using numbers**

Read aloud each number that your instructor shows you. (Numbers will include dates, prices, measurements, etc.)

1.

2.

3.

4.

5.

ACTIVITY 26 **Describing charts and graphs**

Bring to class a pie chart or bar graph from a magazine or newspaper, and talk about the information that it shows.

ACTIVITY 27 **Talking on the telephone**

Following the instructions that your instructor gives you, call her or him on the telephone and leave a message.

Speaking Evaluation Checklist

Your instructor may use the following checklist to assess your speaking in class activities and/or in the Speaking Test.

Speaking evaluation	OK	Needs work	Example
Listening			
► understood question			
Content			
► answered correctly			
Language use			
► expressed ideas clearly			
► used language from chapter			
Pronunciation			
► clear & comprehensible			
► not too fast or slow			
► loud enough			
Nonverbal communication			
► appropriate eye contact			
► correct posture			

W E B   P O W E R

You will find additional exercises related to the content in this chapter at **http://esl.college.hmco.com/students**.

3

Forbidden Food

ACADEMIC FOCUS: NUTRITION AND SOCIAL SCIENCES ▶ SOCIOLOGY/ANTHROPOLOGY

Academic Listening and Speaking Objectives

In this chapter, you will work individually, in pairs, and in small groups to:

- ▶ **Become familiar with the USDA's food guide pyramid and discuss food choices**
- ▶ **Learn new abbreviations and symbols to use in your notes**
- ▶ **Use your dictionary for pronunciation**
- ▶ **Make your lecture notes visual by using concept maps**
- ▶ **Listen for reduced forms of function words**
- ▶ **Learn academic phrases with *and***
- ▶ **Read aloud decimal numbers, fractions, e-mail addresses, and URLs**
- ▶ **Use comparative and superlative forms**
- ▶ **Interpret information in a table**
- ▶ **Compose and send an e-mail message**

Part 1

Nutritionists at the United States Department of Agriculture, or USDA, have determined that we need to eat a variety of foods in order to be healthy. They recommend that every day we eat a certain number of servings from different food groups. To help us remember what we should eat, they have created the Food Guide Pyramid (see Figure 1). The lecture in this chapter, "Forbidden Food," is about food as it relates to culture.

▷ Getting Ready for the Lecture

Food Guide Pyramid

A Guide to Daily Food Choices

Figure 1

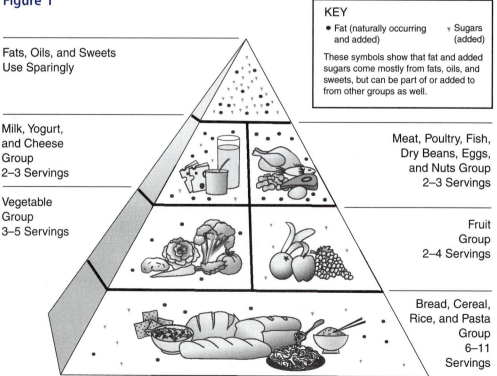

Fats, Oils, and Sweets
Use Sparingly

KEY
● Fat (naturally occurring and added)   ▾ Sugars (added)

These symbols show that fat and added sugars come mostly from fats, oils, and sweets, but can be part of or added to from other groups as well.

Milk, Yogurt, and Cheese Group
2–3 Servings

Meat, Poultry, Fish, Dry Beans, Eggs, and Nuts Group
2–3 Servings

Vegetable Group
3–5 Servings

Fruit Group
2–4 Servings

Bread, Cereal, Rice, and Pasta Group
6–11 Servings

Source: US Department of Agriculture/US Department of Health and Human Services

ACTIVITY 1   Understanding the food pyramid

To prepare for the sociology lecture that you will hear later in this chapter, look at the food pyramid and answer the following questions. (Remember to use the roles you learned in Chapter 1, Activity 12, page 14.)

1. How many categories of food, or food groups, does the pyramid represent?
2. Why do you think nutritionists chose a pyramid shape for their food guide?
3. In which groups are foods that provide protein? Carbohydrates?
4. What food group is at the top of the pyramid? From the context, can you guess the meaning of *sparingly*?
5. What does *poultry* mean?
6. In which category would you put soy products, such as tofu or bean curd? Why?
7. As a group, choose a popular food, e.g., pizza or a taco. Divide/separate the food into its components, or parts, and classify each in one of the food groups from the pyramid, giving the number of servings.

Food	Components	Food Group	Servings
Example:			
cheeseburger	hamburger	meat	1
	bun	bread	2
	cheese	milk	1

ACTIVITY 2   Discussing food choices

The lecture in this chapter is about food choices and foods that are taboo, or forbidden to eat. To get ready for the lecture, discuss your answers to the following questions with a group.

1. Are there foods that you would never eat together? If so, what?
2. Is there something you never eat for breakfast/lunch/dinner? Explain.
3. Are there foods that you would never eat in the summer? Winter? If so, give examples.
4. Is there any kind of meat that you never eat? If so, what kind?

STRATEGY

Reduced Form of Function Words

In Chapter 1, you learned that when professors are speaking, they stress the important words. These words are called *content words* because they contain the important ideas. On the other hand, words that are **less** important are reduced; they are not pronounced completely or clearly. These are called *function words*; they are necessary for grammar, but not important in the speaker's message. In the following example sentence, the stressed syllables of the content words are in **bold** print:

> The **lec**ture in this **chap**ter is about **food choi**ces and **foods** that are ta**boo.**

Three function words often reduced are *and*, *of*, and *them*. *And* is reduced to *'n*, *of* is reduced to *uh*, and *them* is reduced to *'um*, often written *'em*.

What You See Written	What You Hear Pronounced
bacon and eggs	*ba*con *'n* **eggs**
half and half	*haf 'n* **haf**
a lot of energy	*uh* **lot**ta energy
a number of studies	*uh* **number** *uh* **studies**
look at them	**look** at *'um*
a lot of them	*uh* **lot** of *'um*

🎧 **ACTIVITY** **3** **Hearing content and function words**

Listen to the following sentences from the lecture, and fill in the blanks with the words you hear. (The ellipsis, or . . . , indicates that part of the sentence is missing.)

> **Example:** . . . with a specific meal, and with a ___time___
>
> of ___day___.

1. . . . avoid certain foods, in particular, certain _____ of

_____?

2–3. . . . food choice as a _____ of _____, then

discuss the _____ of _____ meat taboos,

and finish . . .

4. . . . associated with _____ and _____ social classes.

Listen to the following sentences from the lecture. What does "them" (or "um") refer to?

5. _____

6. _____

STRATEGY

Academic Phrases with *And* (*'n*)

Many phrases with the reduced *and* are related to food, e.g., *salt 'n pepper, cream 'n sugar, peanut butter 'n jelly*. Others are academic, e.g., *research 'n development*. These are often set phrases; in other words, the same words always go together in the same order. They often include antonyms, or words with opposite meanings.

    [**NOTE:** When a word has more than 1 syllable, only part of the word is in bold.]

        Examples: *sup**ply** and de**mand***
                        ***rules** and regulations*
                        black** and **white
                        do's** and **don'ts
                        ups** and **downs
                        true** and **false
                        *lost and **found***

    Remember that when you pronounce these phrases *and* is pronounced as a reduced *'n*.

ACTIVITY 4 **Completing academic phrases**

Complete the following phrases with the words from the list.

Then write the number of the phrase next to the correct sentence.

Look at #1 as an example.

demand	have-nots	negative	question	research
don'ts	minus	pros	reaction	trial

1. _____*pros*_____ and cons

2. _____ and error

3. supply and _____

4. _____ and answer

5. summary and _____

6. _____ and development

7. haves and _____

8. positive and _____

_____ **a.** One type of assignment that professors give is a _____.
Students read something and they have to write the main points,
in addition to their personal opinion of the reading selection.

__1__ **b.** If you consider both sides of an argument, those that are for it
and those that are against it, you are discussing the _____.

_____ **c.** We often solve problems through _____. We try one possible
solution, and if that doesn't work, we try another and another,
until we find one that works.

_____ **d.** The field of economics teaches us that the price of an item, for
example, beef, is affected by the law of _____. In other words,
the price depends on how much beef is available and how many
people want to buy it.

_____ **e.** Companies spend a lot of time and money on studying and
testing a product before they actually put it on the market. This
part of a company's business is called _____.

_____ **f.** When we compare rich and poor people, we often call them the _____.

_____ **g.** You shouldn't interrupt the speaker now. There will be a _____ session at the end of the speech.

STRATEGY

Using Abbreviations and Symbols

Note-taking is individual, and everybody has her/his own unique abbreviations and symbols. However, there are some that are standard, i.e., a lot of people use them. One technique that is used in English is to delete all of the vowels in a word and include only the consonants, e.g., *hmwrk* for *homework*. Another technique is to write only the beginning of a word, for example, *abbrev* for *abbreviation*. Here are some other examples of common abbreviations and symbols:

Word/Idea You Hear	Symbol/Abbreviation You Write
with	*w/*
without	*w/o*
at	*@*

Try completing the list of examples with these symbols and abbreviations:

→   *bec/'cuz   lrn   nat'l   ↑   grp   ↓   int'l   assoc   avail   trad'l*

increase, high, upper, . . .

decrease, low, lower, . . .

cause(s), results in, . . .

national

international

traditional

because

available

associate, association

learn

group

ACTIVITY 5 **Using abbreviations and symbols**

Listen to parts of the lecture and complete the following notes by writing abbreviations and/or symbols. Feel free to use your own.

Example: humans: big need for protein ___bec. of___ brain

1. Humans: omnivores, but eat fraction of _____ food

2. later we _____ foods _____ other foods, . . .

3. _____ level of socialization, food = symbol of status (social class), gender(sex), _____ membrshp, e.g. relig.

4. meat taboos: most from _____

5. Hindus Buddhists: _____ (no red meat, chicken, or fish)

STRATEGY

Words from the Lecture

To understand the lecture in this chapter, "Forbidden Food," you need to know the meanings of the words in Activity 6. Many of these words are found on the Academic Word List, which means they are used frequently in a variety of academic texts. In other words, you are going to see and hear these AWL words in your other classes—no matter what your major—so you should know them.

In addition to the vocabulary in the list, the professor explains several other new words during the lecture. These are:

edible and inedible	fasting
social status	taboo
gender	sacred

ACTIVITY 6 **Expanding your vocabulary**

Match the definitions from the list with the words in bold print by writing the corresponding letter in the correct space. Look at #1 as an example.

a. The act of eating or drinking something; a quantity of something eaten.

b. Capable of being obtained; at hand and ready to use.

c. To break down (food) chemically into materials that the body can use as nourishment.

d. Small animals with a soft, long, rounded body and no backbone, or spine.

e. To act in response to something.
f. Filled with feelings of sickening dislike or extreme distaste.
g. Something that represents something else by association, resemblance, or custom.
h. The act of forbidding by law or authority; ban.
i. Tame or domesticated (used with animals); not wild.
j. The act of a person eating the flesh, or body, of other humans.
k. To refuse to accept something.
l. A general direction or tendency; vogue.
m. The act of not eating, especially for religious reasons.

1. __b__ Although there is a lot of food **available** to humans, we choose to eat only a small part of it.

2. _____ Table 1 compares the **consumption** of meat in different countries around the world.

3. _____ People in desperate situations, such as the plane crash in the Andes Mountains that was described in *Alive!*, have survived because of **cannibalism**.

4. _____ The human body starts to **digest** food as soon as it enters the mouth.

5. _____ My roommate was **disgusted** when she found a dead mouse in her shoe.

6. _____ One of the latest food **trends** is to eat more ethnic foods, that is, food from different countries.

7. _____ The dog is considered a **domestic** animal, but its relative, the wolf, is not.

8. _____ State and federal buildings in this country have a **prohibition** on smoking.

9. _____ When you go fishing, don't forget to take some **worms** for bait—the fish love 'em!

10. _____ How did your mother **react** when you told her that you were cooking worms for dinner?

11. _____ We offered the dog some food, but he **rejected** it.

12. _____ An expensive car such as a Mercedes Benz or a BMW is a status **symbol**; in other words, it symbolizes a high social class.

ACTIVITY 7 **Using a dictionary for pronunciation**

Use a dictionary to find the syllable stress patterns of the following words from the Academic Word List that are in the lecture, "Forbidden Food."

Compare your answers with a partner's and practice pronouncing the words.

Remember to tap out the syllables with your fingers, or use some other physical movement to feel the syllables and stress.

Example:

[3-1]	[4-3]	[5-3]
energy energies	energetic	energetically

1.

[___ - ___]	[___ - ___]
consume consumed consumes	consumer consumers consuming consumption

2.

[___ - ___]	[___ - ___]	[___ - ___]
available	unavailable	availability

3.

[___ - ___]	[___ - ___]	[___ - ___]	[___ - ___]
react reacts	reacted reacting reaction reactions reactor reactors	reactivate	reactivation

4.

[___ - ___]	[___ - ___]	[___ - ___]	[___ - ___]	[___ - ___]
symbol symbols	symbolize symbolized	symbolic	symbolizes symbolizing symbolism	symbolically

5.

[___ - ___]	[___ - ___]	[___ - ___]
prohibit prohibits	prohibited prohibiting prohibitive	prohibition prohibitions

6.

[___ - ___]	[___ - ___]	[___ - ___]
domestic domestics	domestically domesticate	domesticated domesticating

7.

[—— - ——]	[—— - ——]	[—— - ——]
reject (n.)	reject (v.)	rejected
rejects (n.)	rejects (v.)	rejecting
		rejection
		rejections

ACTIVITY **8**   **Using academic vocabulary**

Read the sentences in Appendix 1 on page 229 as your partner scans Activity 7 for the correct words to complete them. Do the first four, and then switch.

Example:

Student A (on page 229): *For both Muslims and Jews, eating pork is . . .*

Student B (on page 83): *. . . prohibited.*

 Getting Information from the Lecture

STRATEGY

Taking Notes and Following Directions

To take good lecture notes, you need to listen for and write the important ideas and the supporting details that the professor gives. Do not include ideas that are not related to the main points. Use your notes to study for the test. As you listen to a lecture, you have to decide what to include and what not to include in your notes. This makes note-taking extremely complicated: you're listening, understanding, deciding what to write and not to write, using abbreviations and symbols in your notes—all while the professor continues speaking!

When it's time to take the test on the lecture material, you need to read and follow the directions carefully. Students often miss points on exams because they fail to follow the directions. Read and follow the directions for Activity 9. How many things do you have to do in order to complete the activity?

ACTIVITY 9 Understanding main ideas and details

*Close your notebooks and listen to the complete lecture, Forbidden Food. As you listen, put a check mark (✓) next to the ideas that are discussed in the lecture, put an **o** next to those that are **not** discussed, and circle the letter of the best title for the lecture.*

1. _____ The brain and its need for protein

2. _____ Why we eat what we eat

3. _____ Why we eat meat

4. _____ Food choices and meat avoidance

5. _____ Religious and social taboos

STRATEGY

Making Your Notes Visual

In Chapter 1, you learned that notes include important ideas. They also include relationships between those ideas. You can show those relationships in an outline, as you saw in Chapter 2, or you can try making your notes more visual by using concept maps. Concept maps use circles, lines, arrows, and pictures—not just words. Each circle represents a main idea, or concept, and the lines connected to the circle contain related details. Look at the example of a concept map in Activity 10. Do you understand what the notes mean?

ACTIVITY 10 Completing a concept map

Listen to the lecture again and fill in the details in the spaces provided in the concept map on page 86. The circles represent main ideas, and the lines connect the details that are related to the main ideas.

Concept map

Humans
Big need for protein
_____
brain

Today, why meat taboos?
food choice = part of culture

$\frac{1}{5} - \frac{1}{4}$ _____ for brain

dairy food, _____

Humans. Omnivores but eat fraction of _____ food

ex. of kid + _____

learn @ early age what's
_____
for cultural reasons only
(socialization)

We ____ foods ____ other foods,
w/meals, w/special occasions.
____ bacon + eggs for brkfst,
cake for birthday

@ ____ level of socializ'n, food =
symbol of status (social class),
gender (sex), ____ membrshp, e.g. rel.

other reasons for taboos: ex: fasting   ex: _____   ex: jal. pepper
-domestic animals, e.g. cats,
we see as _____
-cockroaches, snakes, seen as
disgusting even tho
may taste _____

Islam + Judaism.
no pork (pig unclean)

Hinduism. no beef
(cow _____)

meat taboos = ban frm social tradition,
most from _____

Hindus + Buddhists.
_____ (no red
meat, chicken, or fish)

Forbidden Food

QUIZ _____

New office hours _____

ACTIVITY 11 Concept mapping

Listen to this mini-lecture; it is the last part of the professor's lecture on forbidden foods. Fill in the concept map with your own notes—remember to use symbols and abbreviations.

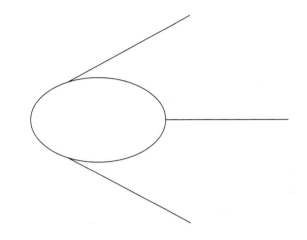

▷ Recognizing Teacher Talk

At the end of the lecture, the professor quickly mentions a change in her or his office hours and says something about a quiz. This is important information, but it's often given very fast, so students miss it. Make sure that you pay careful attention to these announcements.

ACTIVITY 12 Understanding teacher talk

Did you write down the information the professor gave at the end of the lecture? If not, listen again and answer these questions. If so, answer the questions by looking at your notes.

1. When is the quiz?

   _____

2. When are the professor's new office hours?

   _____

3. Is this change in office hours only for next week?

   _____

▼ Take Care of Your Health

To be successful, you need to take care of your health—not just your physical health, but your emotional health, too. Diet, exercise, sleep, and good friends—everything is related and important to your well-being. If you suffer in one area, it affects another. For example, if you don't get enough sleep, you can't concentrate in class.

 ## Using Your Lecture Notes

STRATEGY

Summarizing the Lecture

As you saw in Chapters 1 and 2, if you can summarize the lecture in your own words, either in writing or speaking, then you are demonstrating that you know the material, especially if you can talk about the lecture several days after you have studied your lecture notes. One technique is to write the main points and the keywords on a note card, or 3 x 5 (*three by five*, 3 inches by 5 inches) card, and practice summarizing the lecture looking at the card.

ACTIVITY 13 Summarizing the lecture

1. For five minutes, quietly study your lecture notes from Activities 10 and 11.
2. Then close your book and notebook. With a partner, take turns summarizing the lecture.
3. Speak for two minutes, and then listen to your partner continue for two minutes.
4. Continue with two-minute turns until you have finished saying all the information you remember.

Part 2

▷ Looking at Language

Fractions and Decimals

In Chapter 2, you learned how to read cardinal and ordinal numbers aloud. In this chapter, we are going to study fractions, numbers that can be written ⅗, and decimals, or fractions of 10 (or a power of 10) that are written with a decimal point.

In the following examples, the stressed syllables are in **bold**.

Fractions

When You See ...	You Say ...	
$1/10$	one **tenth**	
$1/4$	one **fourth** or one **quarter**	
$1/3$	one **third** or a **third**	
$1/2$	one **half** or a **half**	
$2/3$	two **thirds**	
$3/4$	three **fourths** or three **quarters**	
$5/8$	five **eighths**	
$9/10$	nine **tenths**	
$1\frac{1}{2}$	one 'n a **half**	('n: reduced *and*)

Decimals

When You See ...	You Say ...	Or ...
.1	point **one**	one **tenth**
0.25	**ze**ro point two **five**	**twen**ty-five **hun**dredths
.30	point three **oh**/**ze**ro	**thir**ty **hun**dredths
0.5	zero point **five**	five **tenths**
.66	point six **six**	**six**ty-six **hun**dredths
.75	point seven **five**	**sev**enty-five **hun**dredths
.605	point six **oh**/**ze**ro five	six **hun**dred five **thou**sandths
.9	point **nine**	nine **tenths**
1.5	one point **five**	one 'n five **tenths**

Don't confuse a **fraction**, one number, with a **rate**, the relationship between two numbers, for example, *35 mph = thirty-five miles per hour* or *thirty-five miles an hour*; and *an interest rate of 12%/year = twelve percent per year* or *twelve percent a year*.

ACTIVITY 14   Reading numbers in a table

Face your partner and look at Appendix 1 on page 230. Ask and answer questions to complete the information in the table on the next page.

Example 1:

Student A (on page 230): *What was the per capita[1] meat consumption in the United States in 1993?*

Student B (on page 91): *(It was) one hundred (and) eighteen kilograms.*

Student A writes (in table): 118

Example 2:

Student B: *What is the projected[2] annual growth of meat consumption in India from 1993 to 2020?*

Student A: *(It is) three point three percent per year.*

Student B writes: 3.3

1. *per capita* = per person
2. *projected* = future

Table 1

Consumption trends of meat, past and projected to the year 2020				
Region	**Per capita meat consumption (kg)**			**Annual growth of meat consumption (percent/year) 1982–1993**	**Projected annual growth of meat consumption (percent/year) 1993–2020**
	1983	**1993**	**2020**		
United States	107	118	114	1.8	0.6
China	16	33	63	8.3	3.2
India	4	4	7	3.1	
Other East Asia	22	44	70	5.4	2.6
Other South Asia	6	7	10	5.4	3.3
Southeast Asia	11		28	5.4	3.6
Latin America	40	46	57		2.2
WANA	20	20	23	2.6	2.7
Sub-Saharan Africa	10	9	11	2.1	3.4
Developing world	15	21	31	5.3	2.9
Developed world	74	78	81	1.2	
World	30	34	40	2.8	1.8

"Meat" includes beef, pork, mutton and goat, and poultry. WANA is Western Asia and North Africa.

POWER GRAMMAR

Comparative and Superlative Forms

Tables and graphs give numerical information in order to make comparisons. In order to make comparisons in English, we use the comparative and superlative forms. The comparative form is used when comparing two things; the superlative is for the top, or highest, of three or more things (*The best answer is c.*) or the bottom (*The lowest passing grade is a C-.*). Look at the following chart with examples of these forms, and fill in the missing information.

	Regular	Comparative	Superlative
Adjectives (Group 1)	high	higher (than)	the _____
	wide	wider (than)	the widest
	low	_____ (than)	_____
	lazy	lazier (than)	the laziest
	early	_____ (than)	_____
	healthy	_____ (than)	_____
Adjectives (Group 2)	traditional	more/less traditional (than)	the most/least traditional
	unusual	more/less unusual (than)	_____
	responsible	_____	_____
	knowledgeable	_____	the most/least knowledgeable
	confident	_____	_____
	current	_____	_____
	disgusting	_____	_____
Adverbs	closely	more/less closely (than)	the most/least closely
	carefully	_____	the most/least carefully
	clearly	_____	_____
	slowly	_____	the most/least slowly

	Regular	**Comparative**	**Superlative**
Nouns	meat	more/less meat (than)	the most/least meat
	protein	_____	the most/least protein
	occasion(s)	more/fewer occasions	the most/fewest occasions
	symbol(s)	_____	_____
	cholesterol	_____	_____
Irregular adj./adv.	good	_____ (than)	_____
	bad	worse (than)	_____
	far	_____	the farthest

POWER GRAMMAR

Avoiding Common Mistakes

Be careful not to make the following mistakes, which are common. Sometimes we get into bad verbal habits, repeating something over and over again until it sounds right to us, but it's actually incorrect.

Wrong	**Right**	**Explanation**
~~more~~ younger	younger	*Younger* already has the meaning of *more*.
the ~~more~~ highest	the highest	Use either the comparative or superlative form—not both.
the ~~most~~ fastest	the fastest	*Fastest* already means *the most*.
~~more~~ better	better	*Better* already means *more*.

ACTIVITY 15   Correcting errors

Correct the errors (in form and/or meaning) in the following sentences.
Compare your answers with a partner's.

worst
Example: Fried food is the ~~most bad~~ thing you can eat.

1. Haiti is the most poor country in the Western hemisphere.

2. Countries in the developed world are more richer than those in the developing world.

3. In 1993 people in developed countries ate a lot more meat that people in developing countries—almost four times more.

4. An 8.3 percent annual growth rate is much more higher than a growth rate of 0.6 percent.

5. ½ is more than ⅔.

6. Of all the people in the world, Americans consume more meat.

7. French fries have a lot more fat that a baked potato.

8. For a healthy diet, we should try to eat more fried foods and fewer fruits and vegetables.

▷ Academic Speaking Task 1

Interpreting Information in a Table

A table gives the same numerical information as a graph or chart, but it is less visual. Instead of circles, lines, or bars, it has lists of numbers. When looking at a table, graph, or chart, you should follow these steps:

1. Look at the title to see what is being compared;
2. Determine what the numbers represent: percentages? centimeters? miles per hour? dollars?
3. Compare the numbers in the table: Is there a big difference between them? What is the highest number? What is the lowest?
4. Think about what the numbers mean: What are possible explanations for the differences? Who might be interested in using the information to support an argument (e.g., government officials, the meat industry, or farmers)?

Look at the following example:

Table 2

Cancer mortality rates by country, 1983 and 1993				
Country	**Deaths**		**Cancer mortality rate (per 100,000)**	
	1983	**1993**	**1983**	**1993**
Canada	42,864	56,192	135.45	133.36
France	128,920	142,712	146.30	140.65
United States	442,923	529,877	137.17	136.52
El Salvador	995	2062	33.85	58.01
Mexico	30,358	44,867	76.84	81.28
Sri Lanka	4276	NA*	39.47	NA*

NA = not available

The table shows cancer mortality rates in six countries in the years 1983 and 1993. The countries are Canada, France, the United States, El Salvador, Mexico, and Sri Lanka. The table shows the number of deaths from cancer in each country in 1983 and 1993, in addition to the cancer mortality rate, that is, the number of deaths per one hundred thousand people. The highest number of deaths in both years was in the United States, but that is logical because the United States has the biggest population. The lowest number of deaths was in El Salvador, but that is logical, too, because El Salvador has the smallest population.

It is interesting to look at the cancer mortality rates, especially the difference between the developed and the developing countries. The rates of the developed countries were much, much higher than those in the developing countries. For example, in 1983, Sri Lanka had a cancer mortality rate of thirty-nine point four seven. The rate in France was more than three times that: one hundred forty-six point three. The big difference could be related to a lot of things: diet, exercise, or stress. It's also curious that the cancer mortality rates in the developed countries all decreased from 1983 to 1993, but in that same ten-year period, they increased in the developing countries. I'm not sure why.

ACTIVITY 16 **Interpreting information in a table**

In your group, practice talking about Table 1 on page 91 by following the four steps on page 95. Then share your discussion with the whole class.

ACTIVITY 17 **Answering questions about a table**

Face your partner and look at Appendix 1, page 232.

Ask the first five questions about Table 1, page 91 and write the answers your partner gives.

Then switch roles and answer the questions.

Example:

Student A (on page 232): *What was the meat consumption of Latin America in 1983?*

Student B (on page 91): *It was forty kilograms per person.*

Student A writes: 40 kg/person

▽ **Looking at Language**

The Language of the Net: Reading E-mail and Website Addresses

The Net, or Internet, has introduced new language to English, and there are rules that we follow when reading aloud an e-mail or website address. An e-mail address always has the symbol "@" (read *at*), and a website address, called a URL (read *U-R-L*), begins with http://www. (This beginning part is often understood, so people don't even say it.) When pronouncing e-mail addresses and URLs, remember to pause at the end of each part. This helps the other person understand what you are saying.

E-mail addresses
(comma = pause; **bold** print = stressed syllable in thought group)

What You See Written	What You Say
kungpao@aol.com	*kung pa*o, at A-O-*L*, dot *com*
kung_pao@earthlink.net	*kung*, *un*derscore, *pao*, at *earth*link, dot *net*
chiefchef@whitehouse.gov	*chief*, *chef*, at *white* house, dot *guv*
professor.pao@harvard.edu	pro*fes*sor, *dot*, *pao*, at *har*vard, *dot*, E-D-*U*

URLs

What You See Written	What You Say
:	*colon*
.	*dot*
/	*slash*
//	*double slash* (or *slash slash*)
\	*back slash*
~	*tilde* (pronounced *till day*)
_	*underscore*

Examples of URLs:

http://www.nal.usda.gov/fnic	H-T-T-*P*, *co*lon, double *slash*, double U double U *dou*ble U, *dot*, n-a-*l*, *dot*, u-s-d-a, dot *guv*, *slash*, f-n-i-c
http://www.college.hmco.com/ collegesurvival/	W-W-W, *dot*, *co*llege, *dot*, H-M-C-*O*, dot, *com*, *slash*, *col*lege sur*vi*val, slash
http://www.nutrition.org.uk//	H-T-T-*P*, *co*lon, double *slash*, double U double U *dou*ble U, *dot*, nu*tri*tion, *dot*, *org*, *dot*, uk, *dou*ble s*lash*

Domain types

The website of an institution or organization has a main web page called its *homepage.* It has links that you click on to connect to other web pages. The three letters at the end of a URL or e-mail address are called *domain types.* They tell you the type of organization you're dealing with.

What You See Written	What You Say	What It Means
.com	dot *com*	a commercial business
.edu	dot, E-D-*U*	an educational institution
.org	dot *org*	a nonprofit organization
.net	dot *net*	a network
.gov	dot *guv*	a government agency
.mil	dot *mil*	the military

STRATEGY

Thought Groups

The most important thing to remember about the pronunciation of URLs and e-mail addresses is to pause and lower the tone of your voice at the right places—the end of each thought group. If you look at the examples above, you can see that you pause when you see a dot, slash, colon, underscore, or @ symbol. The pauses help the listener to understand the information and to allow time to write the information down.

ACTIVITY 18   Reading URLs and e-mail addresses

Face your partner and practice dictating website and e-mail addresses in Appendix 1 on pages 232–233. Do the first five, and then switch.

Example:

Student A (on page 232): *terry, T-E-R-R-Y, dot aki, A-K-I, at mindspring dot com*

Student B (book closed) writes: terry.aki@mindspring.com

Formal vs. Informal Language: E-mailing

E-mailing, or using electronic mail, is a combination of formal and informal language. It's formal in the way it looks: like a memorandum or a business letter. On the other hand, it is informal in its use of language, which sounds more like spoken than written English.

Look at the format of an e-mail message:

To: rschmidt@eng.cal.edu ◄— Enter, or type in, the e-mail address of the person you're sending the message to.

From: ◄— Your e-mail address will appear here.

cc: ◄— If you want other people to receive your message (*cc* means carbon copy), enter their addresses here.

Re: ◄— Type in the subject of your message here. *Re* means *regarding, or about.* This is like the title of your message.

Greeting

Dear Dr. Schmidt, ◄— Put a space here (use the ENTER/RETURN key)

Body → I need to make an appointment with you ASAP to ask you about next week's quiz. Please let me know when you're available, preferably in the morning. ◄— Keep the body of the message short.

Closing → Thank you, ◄— Be polite.
Karen Rodriguez
from your 11:00 biology class ◄— Give your name & other information to let the instructor know who you are.
Tel. 752-3712

ACTIVITY 19 Analyzing e-mail messages

Work with a partner to compare the e-mail message above with the one below by answering the following questions.

1. How are the two e-mails different? (Compare the greetings, the messages, and the closings.)
2. What's the relationship between Karen Rodriguez and Dr. Schmidt? What about between Karen and Kevin Kiley? How do you know?

To: KKiley@earthlink.net
From: Krodriguez@aol.com
Re: Meeting
hey, sweetie,
i miss you & need to see you asap.
can you meet me tomorrow morning?
love,
karen

▽ Academic "Speaking" Task 2

E-mailing a Professor

Even though e-mail messages are more like spoken than written English, we still follow certain rules, such as using the same format. Other rules that we follow are called Netiquette, a combination of *Net*, the Internet, and *etiquette*, or the rules of proper social behavior. Four rules of Netiquette are:

1. Keep your message brief and about one topic;
2. Be careful with your language (Don't write anything that you wouldn't want your mother to read);
3. Use small-case letters unless you want to SHOUT (upper case, or capital letters, are the equivalent of shouting); and
4. If you don't know the person you are e-mailing, say who you are in the body of the message and tell the person why you are writing.

Example:

> **To:** C.Krech@mdc.edu
> **From:** Tatyana@hotmail.com
> **Re:** Excused absence
>
> Dear Professor Krech,
>
> I am in your Writing IV class, MWF at 11:00. I need your signature on a form because I am on the school volleyball team and I am going to be absent from class. Can I stop by your office tomorrow morning?
>
> Sincerely,
> Tatyana Sidorov

ACTIVITY 20 E-mailing a professor

E-mail your professor saying that in the last class you missed the information about her or his office hours. Ask when you can go to her/his office this week.

Part 3

ASSESSING YOUR LISTENING AND SPEAKING SKILLS

▷ Getting Ready for the Test: Self-Assessment

ACTIVITY 21 **Evaluating your skills**

Evaluate yourself on the following skills by putting a check mark (✓) in the column that best describes how you feel you can do each. For every check mark in the third column, go back and practice before you take the test.

Listening I can:	Great	OK	Need to practice
1. use more abbreviations & symbols in my notes			
2. hear content words & reduced forms of function words			
3. anticipate academic phrases with *and* (e.g., *supply & . . .*)			
4. understand & use new vocabulary			
5. listen for important information given by a professor			
6. use a dictionary to find the pronunciation of new words			

Speaking I am able to:	Great	OK	Need to practice
1. describe the USDA food pyramid			
2. read numbers in a table, including fractions & decimals			
3. interpret information in a table			
4. make comparisons, using the comparative & superlative			
5. read e-mail & website addresses aloud			
6. compose & send an e-mail message			
Study skills I am able to:	Great	OK	Need to practice
1. listen to a sociology lecture & take notes			
2. use a concept map in my note-taking			
3. use my notes to summarize a lecture			
4. take care of my health			
5. follow multi-step directions			
6. have a positive attitude			

▷ Chapter Test

To evaluate your progress, your instructor may ask you to do some or all of the following activities for the chapter test.

Listening Test Activities

ACTIVITY 22 **Taking notes**

Listen to the following sentences and complete the notes, using abbreviations and mathematical symbols. Do not write out the words—this is not a dictation.

You hear: *Use abbreviations and mathematical symbols.*

You write: use *abbrev. + math.* symbols

1. table: ↑ meat _____ _____

2. our relat. _____ domest. animals = _____

3. _____ levels satur'd fat + chol. assoc. _____ cancer, stroke, hrt. disease

4. ↓ food trend, begin. _____ cent. = variety of ethnic foods now

   _____, _____ in rests

5. more vegans _____ care abt nutrition, ethics, + _____

ACTIVITY 23 **Using numbers, URLs, and e-mail addresses**

Listen to the following and write what you hear, using numbers, symbols, and abbreviations.

1. _____

   _____

2. _____

   _____

3. _____

   _____

4. _____

_____

5. _____

_____

6. _____

_____

ACTIVITY 24 Completing academic phrases with *and*

Complete the phrases you hear by giving the missing words. (Your instructor may ask you to write or say the complete phrase aloud.)

1.

2.

3.

4.

5.

ACTIVITY 25 **Interpreting information in a table**

Look at Table 2 (page 95), and answer the questions you hear. (Your instructor may ask you to answer orally or in writing.)

You hear: *How many people died of cancer in El Salvador in 1983?*

You answer: *Nine hundred ninety-five people died.*

1. _____

2. _____

3. _____

4. _____

5. _____

6. _____

Speaking Test Activities

ACTIVITY 26 **Talking about the food guide pyramid**

Answer questions that your instructor asks about the food guide pyramid and your own daily food choices.

ACTIVITY 27 **Talking about the lecture**

Answer questions that your instructor asks about the lecture, "Forbidden Food," and food taboos in your own family.

ACTIVITY 28 **Reading website and e-mail addresses**

Read aloud the website and e-mail addresses that your instructor shows you.

ACTIVITY 29 **Using comparative and superlative forms**

Make comparisons about the information that your instructor shows you.

ACTIVITY 30 **Interpreting information in a table**

Talk about the information given in a table from a magazine or local newspaper.

Speaking Evaluation Checklist

Your instructor may use the following checklist to assess your speaking in class activities and/or in the Speaking Test.

Speaking evaluation	OK	Needs work	Example
Listening			
▶ understood question			
Content			
▶ answered correctly			
Language use			
▶ expressed ideas clearly			
▶ used language from chapter			
Pronunciation			
▶ clear & comprehensible			
▶ not too fast or slow			
▶ loud enough			
Nonverbal communication			
▶ appropriate eye contact			
▶ correct posture			

WEB POWER

You will find additional exercises related to the content in this chapter at http://esl.college.hmco.com/students.

Bacteria
Burgers

ACADEMIC FOCUS: MATH AND BUSINESS

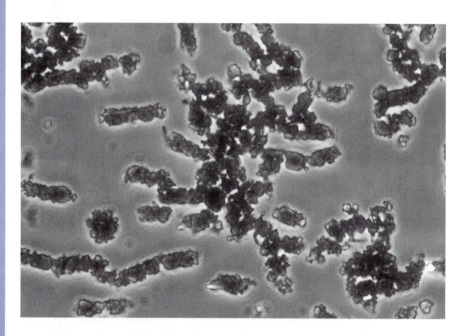

Academic Listening and Speaking Objectives

In this chapter, you will work individually, in pairs, and in small groups to:

- ► Become familiar with a case study in business
- ► Learn new abbreviations and symbols to use in your notes
- ► Understand some commonly used initials and acronyms
- ► Guess the meanings of words from the context
- ► Recognize signal words
- ► Synthesize information from different sources
- ► Use the language of mathematics
- ► Practice presentation skills: eye contact, posture, and voice clarity

Part 1

EFFECTIVE ACADEMIC LISTENING

This chapter's lecture is about a case study. Business courses use case studies to teach about different factors that contribute to a company's success or failure. A case study is a detailed study of a company; students analyze facts about the company to learn what actions help and hurt its success.

▷ Getting Ready for the Lecture

ACTIVITY 1   Talking about business

To get ready for the lecture, see what you know about the following cases. Here are some facts about well-known companies. Fill in the blank with the correct name from the list.

AOL	Honda	Microsoft	Starbucks
Coca-Cola	Jack in the Box	Nike	Toyota
Gap	McDonald's	Proctor & Gamble	Wal-Mart

1. _____ gives millions of dollars in cash and software to charities.

2. _____ and _____ started selling electric *hybrid*[1] cars, which not only pollute the air less than other cars, but also use less gas.

3. _____'s CEO reported to *investors*[2] in the 2001 annual report that their *stocks*[3] increased in value and that the company had expanded into producing fruit juices and water.

4. _____'s customers were *charged*[4] for merchandise that they did not order, simply by logging out from their e-mail accounts.

5. _____ has a children's hospital and provides housing in twenty countries for the families of children who need medical care away from their homes.

6. _____ forced its employees to work overtime without pay after they had clocked out.

7. _____, with the help of Magic Johnson, opened in *inner city*[5] neighborhoods in Los Angeles and New York, providing jobs and a meeting place for the people living there.

8. _____ and _____ were accused of running *sweatshops*[6] in Asia, hiring children to work in their factories and paying them very little for their work.

1. *hybrid* = a plant or animal that has parents of different species
2. *investors* = people who put money into a company
3. *stocks* = shares of the ownership in a company that investors buy on the stock market
4. *charged* = billed on their credit cards
5. *inner city* = the older, central part of a city, especially an area that is poor
6. *sweatshop* = a factory where employees work long hours for low wages under poor conditions; illegal in developed countries

LEVELS OF CORPORATE SOCIAL RESPONSIBILITIES

This chapter's case study deals with corporate social responsibilities. Companies, or corporations, exist to make a profit,[1] but in addition they are responsible to their employees, their customers, the environment, and the neighboring communities. The chart that follows gives examples of four kinds, or levels, of corporate social responsibilities: economic, legal, ethical, and philanthropic.

Companies, both large and small, that make a commitment[2] to corporate citizenship do so at all four levels. Needless to say, not all companies make this commitment to social responsibilities.

Economic	Legal	Ethical	Philanthropic
► making money for investors ► providing employment for the local community ► playing an active role in the economy	► paying workers the minimum wage ► providing safe working conditions ► paying workers extra money for overtime	► doing what is morally right ► having a written code of ethics to show a company's commitment to certain principles such as protecting the environment and encouraging diversity	► donating money, time, and services to help others ► employees' volunteering at homeless shelters or schools ► CEO's donating money to local charities

Source: Adapted from Thorne, D., Ferrell, O. C., & Ferrell, L. (2003). *Business and Society*. Boston: Houghton Mifflin Company. pp. 9–12

1. *profit* = money made from doing business after operating expenses have been paid
2. *commitment* = serious promise; obligation

ACTIVITY 2 Making connections

Using the information about corporate social responsibilities and the corporate cases in Activity 1, complete the chart. Look at #1 as an example.

Case	Level of responsibility	Reason
#1	philanthropic + economic	it's good for the community it's good P.R. (public relations) for corp.
#2		
#3		
#4		
#5		
#6		
#7		
#8		

Initials and Acronyms

In English we often use the shortest possible way to say something. One way we do this is by using initials and acronyms. You are going to hear several initials and acronyms in the lecture from this chapter. Look at these examples:

Instead of Saying . . .	We Use the **Initials** . . .
television	*TV*
the United Kingdom	*the UK*

Instead of Saying . . .	We Use the **Acronym** . . .
the Organization of Petroleum Exporting Countries	*OPEC* (said like a 2-1 word)

Organizations such as the military and fields such as computer science have specialized initials and acronyms that only people working in them understand. Here are some common ones that most people know:

General	Education	Business	Government
DJ	BA	CEO	USDA
ID	GPA	VP	FBI
I-95	TBA	IBM	CIA
pj's	PhD	PR	FEMA*

Computers & electronics	Banking	Correspondence (letters & e-mails)	Medicine & chemistry
VCR	ATM	PS	MD
PC	PIN*	cc	H_2O
DVD	IOU	RSVP	TB
RAM*	APR	PO box	MSG

Pronunciation: Word Stress

All of the initials in the list above are stressed on the last syllable (FBI, ID), except for two: *DJ* and *pj's* are stressed on the first syllable.

*acronym (read it like a word—don't read the individual letters)

ACTIVITY 3   **Understanding initials and acronyms**

*Work with a partner to write the meanings of the initials and acronyms
listed above. Use the first one as an example.*

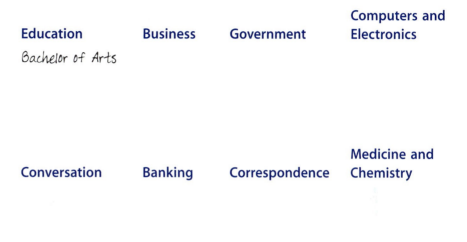

			Computers and
Education	**Business**	**Government**	**Electronics**
Bachelor of Arts			

| | | | Medicine and |
| **Conversation** | **Banking** | **Correspondence** | **Chemistry** |

ACTIVITY 4   **Thinking about initials and acronyms**

*Work with a partner to think of other initials and acronyms that you are
familiar with.*

ACTIVITY 5   **Understanding initials and acronyms**

Listen to the sentences and check (✓) the idea that the speaker is talking about.

You hear: *Is there an ATM near here?*

You check: ___✓___ a bank _____ a school

1. _____ a government form _____ directions for driving

2. _____ a college degree _____ a disease, or sickness

3. _____ a card _____ a computer component

4. _____ a businessman _____ a banker

5. _____ bank account _____ computer

STRATEGY

Using Abbreviations and Symbols

As you learned in Chapter 3, note-taking is individual but there are some standard symbols and abbreviations. Here are some additional ones that you might use in your notes for this chapter's lecture.

Word/Idea You Hear	Symbol/Abbreviation You Write
male(s), men, boy(s)	♂
female(s), women, girl(s)	♀
thousand	K
number	# *or no.* (# is also used for *pound*)

Try completing the list of examples with these symbols and abbreviations.

lbs $ *intro*   *govt*   *regs*   *dept*   *kg*   °   * * *or* ! !

degree

pounds

kilos, kilograms

dollars, money, funds

This is important. This is on the test.

introduction, introduce

department

government

regulations

🎧   **ACTIVITY 6   Understanding abbreviations and symbols**

Listen to the sentences from the lecture.

Choose the notes that represent what was said.

Take time to read the notes carefully before you listen.

Example:

_____ 1993, Wash, ID, Nev. Jack'n Box served 100s o' burgers

__✓___ '93 in Wash, ID, + Nev. 100s sick frm burgers, JinBox

1. _____ events show bus., gov't, + society interrelated

   _____ events occurred in gov't dept.

2. _____ ↑ temps (160°) cause radiation of E. coli

   _____ ↑ temps (160°) + radiation kill E. coli

3. _____ sick people sought help @ Wash.state hlth dept + hosp.

   _____ sick people went to hosp. → staff called state hlth dept

4. _____ J.'n Box had to find place for 28K kg grnd beef

   _____ J.'n Box had to replace 28K lbs. grnd beef

5. _____ Nugent spoke w/ Senate subcmttee, said would follow regs
   for cooking beef

   _____ Nugent spoke in Wash., said wants to change local, state, +
   fed. regs for cooking beef

6. _____ donated $100k rsrch org for kidney probs. in kids w/ E. coli

   _____ donated $100k org studying causes of failure, E. coli

7. _____ also, promised victims their hosp. $ low

   _____ plus, promised $: all hosp. costs for victims

STRATEGY

Words from the Lecture

As in all lectures, to understand the main points, you need to know some of the vocabulary. In this lecture, "Bacteria Burgers," many of the words are found in the following activity. Most of the words are also found on the Academic Word List (AWL), so they are important—not just for this chapter, but for all of your college classes.

ACTIVITY 7 Expanding your vocabulary

Match the definitions from the list with the words in bold print by writing the corresponding letter in the correct space. Be careful—some words are very similar!

Look at #1 as an example. (Note: abbreviation sth. *used for* something)

a. The act of calling back, especially an official order to return.

b. Amounts of money put into businesses in order to earn more money.

c. A careful examination or search in order to discover facts or gain information.

d. Directed the course of (sthg.); managed.

e. Following sthg. else in time or order; succeeding.

f. Got (sthg.) back; regained; regained control over; returned to a normal or healthy condition.

g. In spite of; notwithstanding.

h. Preceding; happening before sthg. else in time.

i. Prepared, treated, or converted by means of a special process, or series of actions.

j. Relating to the central government of the United States.

k. Relating to the management of money.

l. Removed sthg.; took away.

m. Separated (sthg.) into parts in order to determine what it is or how it works; examined (sthg.) in detail.

n. A succession; the order in which things or events occur or are arranged.

1. __f__ After he **recovered** from cancer, Lance Armstrong won the Tour de France six times in a row.

2. _____ Fresh foods are much more healthful than **processed** foods.

3. _____ The chemistry students **conducted** an experiment in the laboratory.

4. _____ The police chief ordered an **investigation** after the first victim died.

5. _____ The newspaper reported the *E. coli* contamination and **subsequent** fear by the public to eat at Jack in the Box.

6. _____ The Ford Motor Company announced a **recall** of 13 million Firestone tires after they were found to be defective, causing a number of accidents.

7. _____ This case study looks at the **sequence** of events that followed the deaths of children infected by the *E. coli* bacterium.

8. _____ Employers are required to pay their workers the minimum wage—it's a **federal** law.

9. _____ When the stock market is down, millions of dollars in **investments** are lost.

10. _____ **Despite** the disabilities of being both blind and deaf, Helen Keller graduated from college and became a writer.

11. _____ Many consumers face **financial** difficulties because they use their credit cards to buy things that they don't have money for.

12. _____ The CEO **analyzed** the situation by looking at all the events and their effects on the company and the public. Then she made a decision.

Source: Definitions from *The American Heritage English as a Second Language Dictionary*. (1998). Boston: Houghton Mifflin.

ACTIVITY 8   Practicing word stress

Choose a word and say it aloud.

Listen to your partner say the stress pattern that he or she hears.

Tell your partner if the stress pattern is right or not.

Do the odd or even numbers, and then switch.

Remember to tap out the syllables with your fingers, or use some other physical movement to feel the syllables and stress.

Example:

[2-1]	[3-1]
process	processes
processed	processing

Student A: *Processed.*
Student B: *3-2. (Three two)*
Student A: *No. I'll say it again: processed.*
Student B: *2-1 (Two one)*
Student A: *Right.*

Before you begin, listen carefully as your instructor reads all of the words aloud.

1.

[3-1]	[4-1]	[4-2]	[5-3]
analyze	analyzes	analysis	analytical
analyzed	analyzing		analytically
analyst			

2.

[2-1]	[2-2]	[3-2]
conduct (n.)	conduct (v.)	conducted
	conducts	conducting
		conductor

3.

[4-2]	[5-2]	[5-4]
investigate	investigated	investigation
investigates	investigating	investigations
	investigator	
	investigators	

4.

[2-1]	[2-2]	[3-2]
recall (n.)	recall (v.)	recalling
	recalls (v.)	
recalls (n.)	recalled	

5.

[2-1]	[3-1]	[3-2]	[4-2]
sequence	sequences	sequential	sequentially
sequenced	sequencing		

6.

[3-2]	[4-2]	[5-2]
recover	recovering	recoverable
recovered	recovery	
recovers		

7.

[2-2]	[3-2]	[3-3]	[4-3]
invest	invested	reinvest	reinvested
invests	investing	reinvests	reinvesting
	investor		reinvestment
	investment		reinvestments
	investments		

8. Notice there are two ways to pronounce most of the forms in Table 8 and that the *i* is also pronounced differently (short when unstressed or long when stressed):

[2-1]	[2-2]	[3-1]	[3-2]	[3-3]	[4-2]
finance	finance	financing	financing	financier	financially
financed	financed	finances	finances	financiers	
			financial		

ACTIVITY 9 Using academic words

Ask the questions in Appendix 1 on page 233, as your partner scans Activity 8 for the correct words to use in the answers. Do the first four and then switch.

Example:

Student A (on page 233): *If there's a dangerous problem with a new product, what does the company have to do?*

Student B (on page 121): *It has to recall the product.*

▽ Getting Information from the Lecture

STRATEGY

Listening for Signal Words

When instructors are lecturing, they often use signal words to indicate the relationship between ideas. These words are like traffic signals: they warn you about what is coming. Recognizing signal words helps you become a better listener and note-taker, because you know what to listen for.

What You Hear	What You Should Expect to Think and Do
1. *For example,…* *For instance,*	The professor just made a point and now he or she is giving an example. Write it in your notes.
2. *In contrast,…* *However,…* *On the other hand,…* *Despite/In spite of…*	Here comes some information that is different from, or in opposition to, what the professor just said. Listen and write it down.
3. *In turn,…* *Consequently,…* *As a result / consequence,…* *Therefore/Thus,…* *Because (of)…*	The professor is explaining a cause-effect relationship. He or she just gave the cause and now he or she is going to give the effect(s). Write → to show the cause-effect relationship.
4. *Before/After…when…* *Then/Next/After that,…* *Subsequently,…* *Later, Eventually…* *Finally,…*	The lecture is about a time sequence, so you will need to know what happened when. Listen for dates, years, and other time expressions. Write them down!

ACTIVITY **10** Listening for signal words

*Listen to parts of the lecture and check (✓) what you should expect to think and/or do. Be sure to read the choices carefully **before** listening.*

You hear: *Now generally, E. coli bacteria are harmless; however, this particular kind of E. coli, 0157:H7, is . . .*

_____ The instructor is going to give an **example** of how harmless *E. coli* is.

____✓____ Now the instructor is going to explain how this kind of *E. coli* is **not** harmless.

1. _____ The **time** sequence is going to be important.

_____ Now the professor is going to give **examples** of different kinds of beef.

2. _____ A **different** subject is coming—the health department—in **opposition** to what the people did.

_____ A **cause-effect** relationship: listen for what the health department did as a result.

3. _____ A **cause-effect** relationship: listen for what the USDA did because of what it found.

_____ Listen for an **example** about the local health department.

4. _____ Listen for **differences** between Jack-in-the-Box management and Domino's Pizza.

_____ Listen for what happened next in the management crisis— **time sequence** and **cause/effect** are important.

5. _____ Here comes information in **opposition** to, or **different** from, something that's morally right.

_____ Here comes an **example** of how the company president did something morally right for the people who got sick.

ACTIVITY 11 **Understanding the main idea**

Listen to the following sentence from the beginning of the lecture. It tells you what the lecture is going to be about. Put a check mark (✓) by the sentence that best describes the topic of the lecture.

1. _____ compare Jack in the Box with other companies and the *E. coli* crisis

2. _____ classify the type of crisis management used by Jack in the Box

3. _____ explain what the Jack-in-the-Box company did to deal with a crisis

4. _____ describe the relationship among business, government, and society

ACTIVITY 12 **Understanding details**

Listen to the lecture and put the events in the correct sequence by writing the letter of the event under the correct domino.

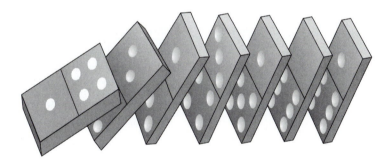

___ ___ ___ ___ ___ ___ ___

a. bacteria spread in ground beef
b. beef is delivered to Jack-in-the-Box restaurants
c. beef is recalled
d. CEO deals with crisis
e. USDA finds *E. coli* in hamburger
f. health department is notified
g. people eat hamburgers and get sick

S T R A T E G Y

Guessing Meaning from Context

When we listen to a lecture, we don't always understand the vocabulary that is used by the speaker, so we need to make intelligent guesses about the meaning of a word. How do we do this?

► by using the context, or language around the word
► by using cognates, or words that are similar in other languages (e.g., *intestine* in English and *intestino* in Spanish)
► by looking at how the word is used in the sentence (i.e., the grammar)

Let's look at an example (without a dictionary). In the lecture, the professor says,

> *Now generally, E. coli bacteria are **harmless**; however, this particular kind of E. coli, 0157: H7, is so toxic, meaning poisonous, that for some individuals, especially young children and the elderly, . . . can make them deathly ill.*

If you understand *harm,* then it's easy to figure out that *harmless* means *without harm.* If you don't understand *harm,* you need to guess the meaning of *harmless.* You know it's about *E. coli* bacteria. *However* tells you that it is different from, and maybe the opposite of, *toxic,* or *poisonous.* So you can infer that *harmless* means *not poisonous,* or something that's not going to hurt you.

ACTIVITY 13 Guessing meaning from context

Listen to the sentence from the lecture, and guess the meaning of the word. Circle the letter of the best choice: a, b, or c.

You hear: *These bacteria are commonly found on vegetables, fruits, and nuts, and in the intestines of cows and humans.*

Intestines . . .

    a. a type of cow or human

    b. a common vegetable, fruit, or nut

    c. a part of the body
       (You should circle letter *c.*)

1. *Huge . . .*
   a. expensive
   b. financial
   c. very big

   tiny . . .
   a. cheap
   b. psychological
   c. very small

2. *Tiny and microscopic . . .*
   a. very big
   b. very expensive
   c. very small

   a bacterium . . .
   a. an amount of money
   b. an organism
   c. a sickness

3. *Infection . . .*
   a. death
   b. restaurant
   c. sickness

4. *Plant . . .*
   a. organism like a flower
   b. factory
   c. meat or hamburger

   facility . . .
   a. a person
   b. a place
   c. an animal

5. *Sought . . .*
   a. infected
   b. looked for
   c. gave

6. *Thereby . . .*
   a. what happened as a result
   b. when something happened
   c. where something happened

7. *Source . . .*
   a. place of origin
   b. result or consequence
   c. name or kind

8. *Declined drastically . . .*
   a. went down fast
   b. went up slowly
   c. became very popular

9. *Donated . . .*
   a. collected
   b. decided
   c. gave

10. *Exposed . . .*
    a. developed
    b. not protected from
    c. shown

S T R A T E G Y

Choosing a Note-taking Style

You can organize your notes in several ways. As you saw in Chapters 1–3, two styles are outlining and concept mapping. They look different, but they both include the same ideas. Whether you choose outlining or concept mapping, you need to decide how you will organize your notes before the lecture begins.

As you take notes, if you miss part of the lecture, leave a space that you can fill in later. At the end of the lecture, you can ask the professor to clarify what he or she said, or you can ask a classmate for the information that you missed. But don't wait—do it immediately after the lecture! Otherwise, you'll forget.

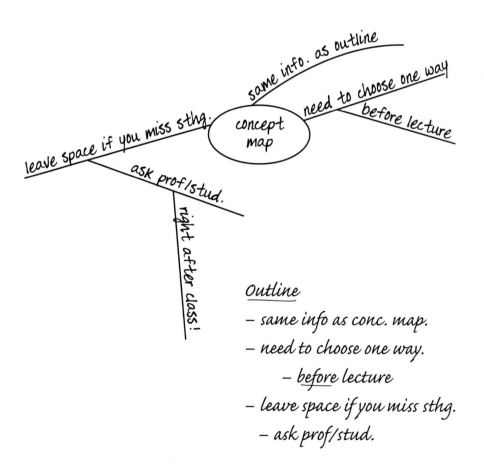

same info. as outline

need to choose one way

before lecture

leave space if you miss sthg.

concept map

ask prof/stud.

right after class!

Outline
- _same info as conc. map._
- _need to choose one way._
    - _before lecture_
- _leave space if you miss sthg._
- _ask prof/stud._

ACTIVITY **14** **Choosing a note-taking style**

Choose either the concept map (begin section at the line near 11:00 and move clockwise, to the right) or the outline format for your notes. Then listen to the lecture and take your own notes in the spaces provided. Remember to use symbols and abbreviations. Notice that the main ideas have been provided.

Concept map

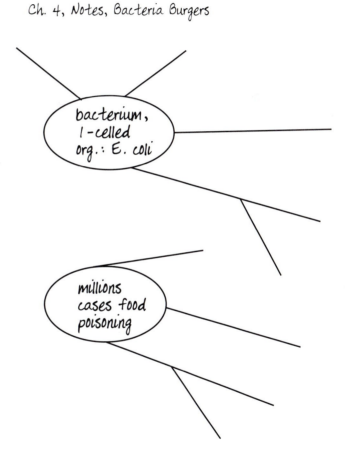

Ch. 4, Notes, Bacteria Burgers

bacterium, 1-celled org.: E. coli

millions cases food poisoning

Today:

Outline

Ch. 4, Notes, Bacteria Burgers

- bacterium, 1-celled org.: E. coli
  - ■
  - ■
  - ■
  - ■
    - ▲

- each year, millions cases of food poisoning
  - ■
  - ■
  - ■

- Today:
  case began in '92, beef proc. plant
  - ■
  - ■
  - ■
    - ▲
  - ■
  - ■
    - ▲
      - ◆
      - ◆

- prez. of J in Box sent team to investig. – J in B found to be source
  of E. coli
  - ■
    - ▲
  - ■
  - ■
    - ▲
    - ▲
  - ■

- effects on company
  - ■
  - ■
  - ■

▷ Using Your Lecture Notes

S T R A T E G Y

Studying with a Classmate

In Chapter 3, you practiced working with a classmate to summarize the class lecture. Another way to study is to work with a classmate and ask each other questions about the lecture and/or textbook. Write questions that you think might appear on a test. One of you can ask about the first half of the lecture, and the other can write questions about the second half.

ACTIVITY **15** **Studying with a classmate**

For five minutes, quietly study your lecture notes from Activity 13.

Write five questions about the lecture that you think would be good test questions.

Close your book and notebook.

With a partner, take turns asking and answering each other's questions.

Part 2

▽ Looking at Language

STRATEGY

The Language of Math

Operations in Math

Business and other university courses use mathematics to make calculations. These mathematical calculations are made using the operations of addition, subtraction, multiplication, and division. Math has its own specialized language, as you can see in the equations below:

What You See	How You Read It	What You're Doing
$1 + 5 = 6$	*One plus five equals[1] six.*	You're adding 5 to 1 for a sum[2] of 6. (or *You're adding 1 and 5 …*)
$12 - 3 = 9$	*Twelve minus three equals nine.*	You're subtracting 3 from 12 for a difference of 9.
$7 \times 2 = 14$ $7 \cdot 2 = 14$ $7(2) = 14$	*Seven times two equals fourteen.*	You're multiplying 7 by 2 for a product of fourteen. (or *You're multiplying 7 and 2 …*)
$8 \div 4 = 2$ $\frac{8}{4} = 2$	*Eight divided by four equals two.*	You're dividing 8 by 4 for a quotient of 2.

Pronunciation: Thought Groups

You saw in Chapter 2 how important it was to pronounce telephone numbers in thought groups. In math, too, thought groups are critical to being understood. Remember to pause and lower the tone (*do, re, mi, …*) of your voice at the end of each thought group. Notice the pauses and stress in the following examples:

$3 + (7 \times 4) = 31$ ***three**, plus seven times **four**, equals thirty-**one***

$(3 + 7) \times 4 = 40$ *three plus **sev**en, times **four**, equals **for**ty*

(The pauses are indicated by a comma (,) and the sentence stress is in **bold**.)

1. You can say *is* instead of *equals*.
2. You can say *for an answer of …* instead of *sum, difference, product,* or *quotient.*

ACTIVITY 16 Reading equations

Listen to your partner read the beginning of one of the equations. Finish reading the correct ending. Do the even or odd numbers.

Example: $(9-6) \div 3 = 1$

$$9-(6 \div 3) = 7$$

Student A: *Nine, minus six divided by three, . . .*
Student B: *. . . equals seven*
Student A: *Right.*

1. $8 + (12 \div 2) = 14$
   $(8 + 12) \div 2 = 10$

2. $(11 - 0)(5) = 55$
   $11 - (0 \cdot 5) = 11$

3. $9 - (4 \times 5) = -11$
   $(9 - 4) \times 5 = 25$

4. $(14 \times 3) - 22 = 20$
   $14 (3 - 22) = -266$

5. $(16 \div 4) - 2.3 = 1.7$
   $16 \div (4 - 2.3) = 9.4$

6. $(3 + 52)(2) = 110$
   $3 + (52)(2) = 107$

7. $(17 - 7) \div 2 = 5$
   $17 - (7 \div 2) = 13.5$

8. $15 + (18 \div 9) = 17$
   $(15 + 18) \div 9 = 3.67$

9. $13(6 + 30) = 468$
   $(13 \times 6) + 30 = 108$

10. $(1 - 25) \div 2 = -12$ *(negative twelve)*
    $1 - (25 \div 2) = -11.5$

ACTIVITY 17 Reading and talking about equations

Listen to your partner and write the equation you hear, using mathematical notation.

Then explain the equation.

Do the first five and switch roles.

> **Example:**
>
> **Student A (on page 234):** *Seven times six equals forty-two.*
>
> **Student B (on this page) writes:** $7 \times 6 = 42$ or $7 \cdot 6 = 42$ or $7(6) = 42$
>
> **Student B says:** *You're multiplying seven by six for a product of forty-two.*

1.

2.

3.

4.

5.

6.

7.

8.

9.

10.

STRATEGY

Fractions and Percentages

Fractions: a fraction is a number that compares part of something with the whole, written. as one whole number, a, divided by another, b: a/b or $\frac{a}{b}$.

What it is	How you write it	How you read it	What it means	When it's used
fraction	1/2 or $\frac{1}{2}$	*one* **half**	1 part of something divided into 2 equal parts	to show how much of the whole
	3/4 or $\frac{3}{4}$	*three* **fourths** *three* **quarters**	3 parts of something divided into 4 equal parts	
	1/5 or $\frac{1}{5}$	*one* **fifth**	1 part of something divided into 5 equal parts	

(Continued)

Percentages: *percent* means *per hundred.* A percentage is like a fraction, but instead of 1 being the whole, 100 is the whole. 50% represents half, 25% is a quarter, or fourth, and 75% is three quarters (or fourths).

What it is	How you write it	How you read it	What it means	When it's used
percentage	50% .50 50/100	*fifty percent*	one half	to show how much of the whole
	75% .75 75/100	*seventy-five percent*	three fourths, 75 parts out of 100	
	20% .20 20/100	*twenty percent*	one fifth, 20 parts out of 100	

ACTIVITY **18**   **Reading fractions and percentages**

Read the first four sentences in Appendix 1 on page 235 while your partner listens and writes the number in the blank. Then switch.

Example:

Student A (on page 235) says: *One kilo is the same as two point two pounds.*

Student B (on this page) writes: One kilo is the same as 2.2 pounds.

1. More than _____ of the illnesses due to food are caused by unknown sources.

2. Among the illnesses due to food, _____ are caused by bacteria, _____ by **parasites**,* and _____ by viruses.

3. More than _____ of the illnesses caused by the dangerous kind of *E. coli* are transmitted through food.

4. Only _____ of the people who are infected with *E. coli* report it, whereas _____ of the hepatitis A cases are reported.

5. Bacteria cause _____ of the deaths associated with food poisoning, but only _____ of the hospitalizations for stomach problems are due to bacteria.

6. Infections with other types of *E. coli* bacteria are _____ as common as those with *E. coli* 0157:H7.

7. Five microorganisms are the cause of more than _____ of the estimated food-related deaths. *E. coli* is one of them, causing _____ of these deaths.

8. Approximately _____ of the estimated 76 million annual cases of food poisoning in the United States are caused by *E. coli*. That's _____ of _____ .

*parasites = organisms that live in or on another species

▷ Academic Speaking Task 1

Solving Math Problems

In many college classes, you have to use math to solve problems. In addition, you have to be able to **talk about** the solutions to the problems and the steps you followed to find the solutions. This is true for business, statistics, computer science, chemistry, and engineering. No matter what the subject, in order to solve problems that involve math, follow these steps:

1. Determine the unknown, or what you need to find (x: the "variable").
2. Decide what kind of problem it is. (Addition? Multiplication?)
3. Translate from English to math by writing an equation.
4. Do the math.
5. Make sure that your answer makes sense.

Let's follow the steps to solve a couple of math problems:

Using operations (addition, subtraction, multiplication, and division)

Word problem: Jin took six credits last semester, and this semester he's taking twice as many credits. How many credits is he registered for now?

1. The unknown, or x, is the number of credits Jin's taking now.
2. I'm going to multiply (*twice* means *two times as many*).
3. I write: $x = 6 \times 2$
4. I do the math: $x = 12$
5. 12 makes sense because it should be more than 6, the number of credits Jin took last semester.

To talk about the steps we followed, we can say:

I decided the unknown was the number of credits Jin's taking now. Then I chose to do multiplication because the problem said "twice as many" and that means "two times." I wrote x equals six times two. After that, I did the math: I multiplied 6 by two for an answer of twelve. Jin is taking twelve credits this semester.

Calculating fractions and percentages

Word problem: The college president announced that because of budget problems, there is going to be a tuition increase of 7 percent. If Lourdes is paying $925 for her tuition, how much more will she have to pay next year?

1. The unknown, or x, is the increase in Lourdes' tuition.
2. I'm going to multiply because in order to figure out percentages and fractions of different numbers, you multiply the number by the fraction or the percentage.
3. I write: $x = 925 \times .07$
4. I do the math: $x = 64.75$
5. That makes sense because I know that 7% of 1000 is 70, and it should be a little less than that ($925 < 1000$).

To talk about the steps we followed, we can say:

I decided the unknown was the increase in Lourdes' tuition. Then I chose to do multiplication because I had to figure out a percentage. I wrote x equals nine hundred twenty-five times point zero seven. Then I did the math: I multiplied nine twenty-five by point zero seven for an answer of 64.75 (sixty-four point seventy-five). Lourdes will have to pay $64.75 (sixty-four dollars and seventy-five cents) more in tuition.

ACTIVITY 19   Using math in business

Follow the steps above to solve these math problems.

After you find the answer, talk about the steps you followed.

Do the even or odd numbers.

1. Your wages are $12 an hour. If you work 35 hours, how much money will you earn before taxes are taken out?

2. You have two jobs. One week your paycheck for the first job is $275, and for the second job, it's $182. After paying your phone bill for $89, how much do you have left?

3. You get a promotion at work, a factory, and your supervisor tells you that you have to divide your workers into teams, with 6 workers on each team. If there are 78 employees in your area, how many teams can you form?

4. Your boss tells you that you have to reduce your business expenses by a tenth. If your average monthly expenses are $460, how much will you have to cut?

5. You work at a company and your boss asks you to take some important clients out for lunch. You go to a nice restaurant, and the server brings you the check for $92. How much do you leave for a tip?

6. You're a sales clerk at a clothing store, and your boss tells you to mark down everything in the store 20 percent and write the new sale prices on the price tags. The first item costs $29.95. What do you write on the new price tag?

7. You're a cashier at a store and the cash register is broken. The sales tax in your state is 7 percent. If a customer has items totaling $54.17, how much will you have to add for tax?

8. You're an accountant at Jack in the Box. The CEO asks you to estimate the amount of money the company lost during the *E. coli* crisis. Legal fees were around two million dollars. Investment losses were approximately $1.5 million. After the beef recall, the company had to purchase new beef for a total of fourteen thousand dollars. One business expert estimated that Jack in the Box lost at least fifty-six thousand dollars in sales. What do you tell the CEO?

▷ Academic Speaking Task 2

Practicing Presentation Skills

In some of your college courses, you will be required to give a presentation in front of the class. When speaking in front of a group of people, you will be evaluated on content (what you say) and presentation (how you say it). In this chapter, you will work on the following presentation skills. These will help you later when you will be expected to give a short speech. They will also help you in everyday communication.

Do's and don'ts for speaking

Eye contact. It's important to look at everyone in the audience, but just like a conversation, you should look at each person for only one to two seconds. If you look at a person for more than five seconds, it's considered rude, and the person will feel uncomfortable. If you don't look at a person at all, it's also impolite.

Posture. You need to stand up straight, hands at your sides when not gesturing,* and relaxed, not tense.

Voice quality. Everyone in the audience needs to hear and understand you, so you need to speak clearly, loudly enough (without shouting), and not too slowly or fast. Pause after each thought group.

For most presentations, or speeches, you will have time to prepare what you are going to say. In this chapter, however, you will have very little time to think about your topic, because you will be thinking about three things: looking at everyone in the audience, standing straight, and speaking loudly and clearly. Your instructor will model good presentation skills by speaking for one minute about one of the topics in the following activity.

*gesture = move your body to communicate sthg.

ACTIVITY **20**   **Practicing presentation skills**

Look at the following topics and think about what you can say about each. Then choose one, stand up in front of the group, and speak about the topic for one minute.

Topics

1. Talk about a fast-food restaurant such as Jack in the Box: What food do they serve? What do you like/dislike about it?
2. Compare two fast-food restaurants.
3. Tell a story about a personal experience with food poisoning.
4. Talk about how to prevent food poisoning.
5. Explain the safety rules and regulations that you have to follow at your job.
6. Explain how one company (or different companies) treated you as an employee.
7. Describe a corporate crisis that you know about.

ACTIVITY **21**   **Being a good listener**

As a member of the audience, answer the following about your classmates' speeches:

1. Did the speaker look at you?
2. Did he or she have good posture?
3. Did he or she speak loudly and clearly enough for you to understand?

STRATEGY

Synthesizing Information

In all your classes, you will get information from different sources, mostly lectures, textbooks, and handouts. This information will be related in some way, and you need to figure out how it is related. In other words, you need to synthesize the information. To use this chapter as an example, you read information about corporate social responsibilities on page 112, and you listened to a lecture about a particular corporation, Jack in the Box. How is the information from the two sources related?

ACTIVITY 22   Synthesizing information

Using your lecture notes and what you remember about corporate responsibilities on page 112, complete the chart. Give an example of how Jack in the Box acted responsibly at each of the levels of corporate social responsibilities.

Level of responsibility	Example: Jack in the Box
economic	
legal	
ethical	
philanthropic	

Part 3

ASSESSING YOUR LISTENING AND SPEAKING SKILLS

▷ Getting Ready for the Test: Self-Assessment

ACTIVITY 23 **Evaluating your skills**

Evaluate yourself on the following skills by putting a check mark (✓) in the column that best describes how you feel you can do each. For every check mark in the third column, go back and practice before you take the test.

Listening I can:	Great	OK	Need to practice
1. understand initials & acronyms (*CEO, ID*)			
2. use more abbreviations & symbols in my notes			
3. understand & use new vocabulary			
4. identify syllable stress patterns [*3-1*]			
5. recognize signal words (*however, consequently*)			
6. guess the meanings of words from the context			
Speaking I am able to:			
1. talk about corporate responsibilities, & explain the Jack-in-the-Box case study			

Speaking (cont.) I am able to:	Great	OK	Need to practice
2. use academic words with the correct stress			
3. read mathematical equations			
4. solve math problems & talk about the solutions			
5. speak in front of an audience with good eye contact, posture, & voice clarity			
Study Skills I am expected to:			
1. predict test questions			
2. listen to a business lecture & take notes			
3. use my notes to study with a classmate			
4. help others understand me			
5. follow the 2-for-1 rule			
6. synthesize information from different sources			

▷ Chapter Test

In order to evaluate your progress, your instructor may ask you to do some or all of the following activities for the chapter test.

Listening Test Activities

ACTIVITY 24 **Using numbers, initials, and vocabulary**

Listen to the following sentences and take notes, using abbreviations and symbols.

1.

2.

3.

4.

5.

ACTIVITY 25 **Understanding the language of mathematics**

Listen to the following and write what you hear, using numbers and math symbols.

1.

2.

3.

4.

5.

6.

ACTIVITY 26   **Understanding abbreviations and symbols**

Listen and choose the correct notes.

1. _____ –1993, Wash, ID, Nev. Jack'n Box served 100s o' burgers

   _____ –'93 in Wash, ID, + Nev. 100s sick frm burgers, JinBox

2. _____ this kind of E. coli super toxic, can kill, esp. kids + elderly

   _____ this kind of E. coli not poisonous, need > 10K to kill s.o.

3. _____ 3 kids died frm E. coli infection

   _____ kids died frm E. coli: 1) 3 in Seattle

                                        2) 2 in Nev.

4. _____ E. coli can destroy bacteria in 2 ways

   _____ 2 ways to destroy E. coli: 1) radiation

                                       2) ↑ temps (>160°)

5. _____ CEO heard of E. coli problem → sent team to investig.

   _____ CEO contaminated by E. coli: spent $$

Speaking Test Activities

ACTIVITY 27   **Understanding and using academic words**

Answer the question you hear by putting a check mark next to the correct word. Then write the syllable-stress pattern for that word. (You may be asked to pronounce and/or use the word, too.)

You hear: *What's another way of saying that you're going to manage or direct an investigation?*

_____ analyze   [___ - ___]

__✓__ conduct   [_2_ - _2_]

_____ invest   [___ - ___]

1. _____ finances   [___ - ___]

   _____ investor   [___ - ___]

   _____ sequence   [___ - ___]

2. _____ analysis   [___ - ___]

   _____ investment   [___ - ___]

   _____ process   [___ - ___]

3. _____ federal   [___ - ___]

   _____ financial   [___ - ___]

   _____ subsequent   [___ - ___]

4. _____ analysis   [___ - ___]

   _____ recall   [___ - ___]

   _____ sequence   [___ - ___]

5. _____ analysis   [___ - ___]

   _____ process   [___ - ___]

   _____ sequence   [___ - ___]

ACTIVITY 28   **Using the language of mathematics**

Read the math equations that your instructor shows you and explain what they mean.

Your instructor shows you: $7 \times 6 = 42$

You say: *Seven times six equals forty-two.*

You're multiplying seven by six for a product of forty-two.

ACTIVITY 29   **Talking about the lecture**

Answer the questions your instructor asks you about the lecture "Bacteria Burgers."

Speaking Evaluation Checklist

Your instructor may use the following checklists to assess your speaking in class activities and/or in the Speaking Test.

Speaking evaluation	OK	Needs work	Example
Listening			
► understood question			
Content			
► answered correctly			
Language use			
► expressed ideas clearly			
► used language from chapter			
Pronunciation			
► clear & comprehensible			
► not too fast or slow			
► loud enough			
Nonverbal communication			
► appropriate eye contact			
► correct posture			

Oral presentation	OK	Needs work	Example
Preparation			
► chose a familiar topic			
Language use			
► expressed ideas clearly			
Voice quality			
► comprehensible			
► not too fast or slow			
► loud enough			
Nonverbal communication			
► appropriate eye contact			
► correct posture & gestures			

WEB POWER

You will find additional exercises related to the content in this chapter at http://esl.college.hmco.com/students.

Canine Colleagues

ACADEMIC FOCUS: ANIMAL SCIENCE

Academic Listening and Speaking Objectives

In this chapter, you will work individually, in pairs, and in small groups to:

- ► Learn about the relationship between dogs and humans
- ► Understand and use some common phrasal verbs
- ► Distinguish between objective and subjective statements
- ► Use your dictionary for pronunciation
- ► Recognize more signal words
- ► Listen for main ideas and details
- ► Guess the meanings of words from the context
- ► Ask questions for clarification
- ► Prepare and practice an oral presentation

Part 1

Many universities offer courses, often interdisciplinary, on the relationship between animals and humans. University College London has a class called Nature and Culture. The University of California at Santa Barbara offers a course, Animals in Human Society. At the University of Pittsburgh, there is a course titled Zoological Philosophy. A similar class, Animals and Ethics, is offered at the University of Alabama. The lecture in this chapter, "Canine Colleagues," might appear in one of these courses.

▷ Getting Ready for the Lecture

ACTIVITY 1   Seeing what you already know

This chapter's lecture is about the close working relationship between dogs and humans. See what you already know about the subject by filling in the blanks with the words from the list. (Hint: three of the words are not used.)

breed	feline	hunting	social
breeds	herd	smell	wolf
cat	herding	species	wolves

Archeologists tell us that dogs, descended from _____ over 10,000 years ago, were the first animals to be domesticated by humans. Like their _____ cousins, dogs are _____ animals, which might explain why they have had such a close relationship with humans for so long.

Throughout history, dozens of dog _____ developed in different parts of the world. Each _____ had different characteristics, so it was trained for a specific use. One way that human beings have used dogs is for _____ . Dogs in general have a much better sense of _____ than humans. For that reason, they are good hunters. Three _____ classified as _____

dogs are the golden retriever, the Labrador retriever, and the beagle.

Golden retriever

Beagle

A second group of dogs helped farmers control the movements of

large numbers of cattle or sheep. A group of cattle or sheep is called a

_____ , and these dogs are known as _____

dogs. They are intelligent, energetic, and hardworking. Two

_____ that belong to this category are the Border collie

and the German shepherd.

In addition to hunting dogs (also known as sporting dogs) and

herding dogs, there are five other canine classifications: hounds, toy dogs,

working dogs, terriers, and non-sporting dogs.

Border collie

German shepherd

Source: O'Neill, A. (1999). *Dogs*. New York: Kingfisher. (p. 10)

POWER GRAMMAR

Phrasal Verbs

Vocabulary in college textbooks is more formal than the words used by professors in lectures. For example, a textbook might use the academic term, *investigate*, but in class, your instructor would say the conversational *find out*. *Find out* is a phrasal verb and it is very common in spoken English.

A phrasal verb is a verb that consists of two or more words, such as *find out*. The first word is a verb, *(find)*, and the second word is a preposition *(out)*. The words function as a whole, or phrase, and have a different meaning from their separate parts. Some common phrasal verbs and their meanings include:

Phrasal Verb	Meaning
1. *find out*	learn, discover (sthg. = something)
2. *take out*	remove (sthg.) that's **inside** sthg. else
3. *take off*	remove (sthg.) that's **on** sthg. else, as in clothing

Work with a partner to complete the list with these phrasal verbs:

check out	*fill out*	*give back*	*hand in*	*hand out*
help out	*leave out*	*look up*	*make up*	*pick up*
put on	*put away*	*turn in*	*turn off*	*turn on*

4. _____ take (sthg.) and record what you're taking (library books, for example)
5. _____ return (sthg.) to its usual place
6. _____ give (sthg.) to an authority
7. _____ cause (sthg.) to begin operation/activity
8. _____ stop the operation/activity of (sthg.)
9. _____ assist (sbdy. = somebody)
10. _____ omit (sbdy./sthg.)
11. _____ search for and find (sthg.) in a reference book
12. _____ submit or turn (sthg.) in
13. _____ distribute or give (sthg.) out
14. _____ complete (a form) by writing required information
15. _____ take (sthg.) with your hand; give (sbdy.) a ride
16. _____ do (an exam/assignment) again or at a later time
17. _____ return (sthg.)

(Continued)

How to Use Phrasal Verbs

In English grammar, there are different kinds of phrasal verbs. This chapter looks at the most common kind, those that are transitive and separable. Let's look at examples of how they work:

Correct	Explanation
1. *Please fill out this form.*	Phrasal verb is not separated; the object is a noun, *form*.
2. *Please fill this form out.*	You can separate the phrasal verb when the object is a noun (*form*).
3. *Please fill it out.*	You **have to** separate the phrasal verb when the object is a pronoun (*it*).

Not correct

4. ~~*Please fill out it.*~~	See Explanation #3.

Correct

5. *Did you pick up Alex?*	See #1 (noun here: *Alex*).
6. *Did you pick Alex up?*	See #2.
7. *Did you pick him up?*	See #3 (pronoun here: *him*).

Not correct

8. ~~*Did you pick up him?*~~	See #3.

This chapter's lecture uses two kinds of phrasal verbs: separable and inseparable. We will study inseparable phrasal verbs in Chapter 6. Two examples of inseparable phrasal verbs are:

USDA <u>stands for</u> United States Department of Agriculture. (meaning: *represents*)

Detector dogs <u>go through</u> extensive training. (meaning: *experience*)

How to Pronounce Phrasal Verbs

In natural speech, phrasal verbs are not usually pronounced slowly and clearly. In addition to reduced forms of pronouns ('*er* for *her*, '*um* for *him/them*), speakers link the words together. If you listen carefully, however, you can hear the stressed syllables of the content words (in **bold**). Listen to your instructor pronounce the following:

What the Person Is Saying	How It Is Pronounced
Please hand them in.	*Please **hand** 'um **in**.*
Did you pick him up?	*Didja **pick** 'um **up**?*
Can you help her out?	*Can ya **help** 'er **out**?*

🎧 **ACTIVITY** **2** **Understanding phrasal verbs**

Listen to the sentences and check (✓) the idea that is closest in meaning to what you hear.

You hear:

My dog went through obedience training.

You check:

___✓___ My dog completed an obedience class.

_____ My dog trained me to throw the ball.

1. _____ I left my dog at the registration desk, which was full of people.

_____ I didn't write some information on my dog's registration form.

2. _____ Stacy found her dog by the mailbox.

_____ Stacy didn't know the sex of her dog.

3. _____ Guide dogs assist people who are blind.

_____ Guide dogs lead blind people outside.

4. _____ I stood up to look at the DEA building.

_____ I used my dictionary to find *DEA*.

5. _____ A detector dog can work in the dark.

_____ Don't turn right if you want to see a detector dog use his nose.

6. _____ Return the video where it belongs after you watch it.

_____ You went away after you watched the video.

7. _____ We have to use our hands to feel our dogs in the class.

_____ We need to write some information and give it to the instructor.

ACTIVITY **3**   **Unscrambling sentences with phrasal verbs**

Unscramble the following words to make a complete sentence. With a partner, practice saying each using the correct sentence stress.

Example: her / off / She / took / watch

She took off her watch. OR *She took her watch off.*

1. but / due / homework / I / in / it / on / on / The / Tuesday / turned / was / Wednesday

2. *beagle* / dictionary / didn't / I / I / in / it / looked / so / the / the / understand / up / word

3. do / final / find / grades / How / our / out / we

4. a / absent / According / can't / for / if / it / make / syllabus / test / the / to / up / we / we're

5. away / calculators / math / our / put / instructor / The / to / told / us

6. a / because / C- / got / I / I / information / left / my / on / out / paper / some

7. After / and / exams / handed / out / pencils / picked / started / students / instructor / the / the / the / their / to / up / write /

8. class / guy / he's / his / in / off / should / sunglasses / take / That / while

9. and / books / hundred / open / out / page / Please / seven / take / them / to / two / your

10. and / by / hand / homework / in / is / it / Make / sure / Thursday / typewritten / your

11. and / beepers / cell / class / during / off / phones / should / Students / their / turn

ACTIVITY 4 **Following directions**

In your group, write three to four more directions, using phrasal verbs if you can.

Take turns reading your directions to your group, who need to do what you say.

> **Example:** *Maria, walk to the board and print your first name. Leave out the last letter.*

(Maria walks to the board and writes *Mari.*)

STRATEGY

Becoming a Critical Listener

As college students and educated adults, we need to be critical thinkers and listeners. That means we shouldn't believe everything that we read or hear. Instead, we should evaluate it before accepting or rejecting it. In order to evaluate information, we consider who says it (the source) and how reasonable it is.

The first step in becoming a critical thinker is to be able to differentiate between objective and subjective statements. Objective statements are not influenced by personal feeling or emotion, whereas subjective statements are based on personal opinion. Here are some other differences:

Objective Statements (Facts)	Subjective Statements (Opinions)
Source	
1. an expert, a person who's disinterested (has no personal interest in the topic)	1. someone who has a personal interest in the topic
2. person presents both sides of an argument	2. person gives only one side of an argument

(Continued)

Objective Statements (Facts)	Subjective Statements (Opinions)
Reasonableness	
3. something generally accepted, considered true	3. something accepted by some, but other people disagree
4. something observable, measurable, and/or provable	4. something showing personal evaluation (*good, bad*) or emotion

Examples: *Tigers and elephants are used in the circus.*

This is an objective statement. It's generally accepted, and we can go to various circuses and observe tigers and elephants.

Animals shouldn't be used in the circus.

This is a subjective statement. The word *shouldn't* tells us that it's an opinion, and it's a statement that some people would disagree with.

 ACTIVITY 5 **Distinguishing between fact and opinion**

Listen to the following statements and take notes.

Write "O" for each objective statement and "S" for each subjective statement. (Hint: Not all the statements are true.)

Compare answers in your group and discuss the reasons for your choices.

You hear:

German shepherds are bigger than beagles.

You write: _____O_____

1. _____

2. _____

3. _____

4. _____

5. _____

6. _____

7. _____

Words from the Lecture

In order to understand the lecture in this chapter, "Canine Colleagues," you need to know the meanings of the words in the following activity. Many of these words are found on the Academic Word List (AWL), which means they are used frequently in a variety of academic texts. In other words, you are going to see and hear these AWL words in your other classes—no matter what your major—so you should know them.

Note: the abbreviation *sthg.* is used for *something*, *sbdy.* for *somebody*, and *esp.* for *especially*.

administration: 1. The act or process of directing the affairs of a business, school, or other institution; management. **2.** The people who manage an institution or direct an organization.

assistance: Help, aid.

blind: Not able to see; sightless.

certified: Guaranteed to be true or valid with an official document.

design: To draw up plans, sketches, or drawings for (sthg.).

detect: To discover or determine the existence of (sbdy./sthg.).

detector(s): A thing that detects, esp. a mechanical, chemical, or electrical device: *a metal detector in an airport.*

disaster: Something that causes great destruction and terrible trouble. *Tornadoes, earthquakes, and floods are natural disasters.*

evaluate: To find out or estimate the value of (sbdy./sthg.); examine and appraise.

evolve(d): 1. To develop (sthg.) gradually. **2.** To develop (a characteristic) by biological evolution.

federal: Relating to a central government, esp. of the United States: *the Federal Bureau of Investigation.*

guide: A person or thing that shows the way, directs, leads, or advises sbdy./sthg.: *a tour guide; a guide to good manners.*

prohibited: Forbidden; banned; not permitted.

rescue: An act of saving (sbdy./sthg.) from danger. *A lifeguard came to our rescue.*

scent: Odor; aroma; smell; perfume.

search: To make a careful examination of (sthg.) in order to find a missing person or thing. -*n.* The act of searching.

survive(d): To stay alive or in existence: *trying to survive in the woods.*

Source: Definitions from *The American Heritage English as a Second Language Dictionary.* (1998). Boston: Houghton Mifflin Company.

ACTIVITY 6 **Expanding your vocabulary**

Fill in the blank with the correct word from the list.

1–2. If you want your dog to work in _____ and

_____ , the dog has to pass a long test.

FEMA will evaluate the dog on its ability to find a person who is

hidden, and you will be tested on your handling of the dog and your

knowledge of the rules.

3. FEMA stands for the Federal Emergency and Management

_____ .

4. Architects _____ buildings.

5–6. A guard dog is trained to bark and bite in order to protect people

and their property. A _____ dog,

however, is trained to be gentle in order to help its handler, who

is usually _____ and needs help getting

around.

7. Could you please help me? I need your _____.

8. All new homes and other buildings are required to have built-in

   smoke _____ .

9. Over thousands of years, dogs have _____

   from wolves.

10. There are different levels of government: the local level, which

    includes cities, towns, and countries; the state level, which is a

    lot bigger; and the _____ level, which

    covers the whole country.

11. Smoking is _____ in this building. If

    you want to smoke, you will have to go outside.

12. Dogs and cats have a better sense of smell than humans. For

    example, after they meet a person, they remember that person

    by her or his _____ .

13–14. Dogs are often used to find people who have _____

    a natural _____ such as an earthquake.

15–16. Professional organizations _____ people

    to see if they are qualified to practice. If they pass, they become

    _____ and receive a license (or certificate).

ACTIVITY **7**   **Using your dictionary for pronunciation**

*Use a dictionary to find the pronunciation of the different forms of the following academic words. (Hint: Some of the forms are **not** in the dictionary.)*

Write the word form in the correct column.

Compare your answers with a partner's and practice pronouncing the words.

Remember to tap out the syllables with your fingers, or use some other physical movement to feel the syllables and stress.

Example: *prohibited* (eight forms)

[3-2]	[4-2]	[4-3]	[5-2]
prohibit	prohibited	*prohibition*	*prohibitively*
prohibits	*prohibiting*	*prohibitions*	
	prohibitive		

1. *design* (six forms)

[2-2]	[3-2]
design	

2. *evaluate* (six forms)

[4-2]	[5-2]	[5-4]
evaluate		

3. *assist* (seven forms)

[2-2]	[3-2]
assist	

4. *administration* (eight forms)

[4-2]	[5-2]	[5-4]	[6-4]
		administration	

5. *evolve* (six forms)

[2-2]	[3-2]	[4-3]	[6-3]
evolve			

ACTIVITY 8 Using academic words

Read the sentences in Appendix 1 as your partner scans Activity 7 for the correct words to complete them. Do the first four and then switch.

Example:

Student A (on page 236): *Administrators want to know how well their instructors are doing in the classroom, so they ask the students to fill out an instructor . . .*

Student B (on page 164): *Evaluation.*

▷ Getting Information from the Lecture

STRATEGY

Listening for Signal Words

At the beginning of a lecture, instructors often indicate what they are going to talk about, how the lecture is organized, and what the important points are. They do this by using signal words. During the lecture, they use other signal words to indicate the relationship between ideas. Recognizing signal words helps you to be a better listener and note-taker, because you know what to listen for and what to write in your notes.

What You Hear	**What You Should Expect to Think and Do**
1. *Three effects of this are . . .*	This is important. Write a list of **three effects** in your notes. Listen for "First," "second," and "third."
2. *There are four reasons for . . .*	Start a list with **reasons:** *1, 2, 3, 4.* Leave space for writing in information later.
3. *Three differences between . . .* *They're similar in three ways . . .*	Here comes an explanation of **differences** or **similarities.** Write 1, 2, 3, and listen for the explanations.
4. *Today we're going to look at five kinds of . . .*	Start a list with **kinds:** *1, 2, 3, 4, 5.* Leave space for writing in information later.

🎧 **ACTIVITY 9 Listening for signal words**

*Listen to the sentences and check (✓) what you should expect to think and/or do. Be sure to read the choices carefully **before** listening.*

You hear:

Three breeds classified as hunting, or sporting, dogs are . . .

You check:

_____ The instructor is going to give 3 reasons for using these breeds.

__✓__ Now the instructor is going to name 3 breeds of dogs.

1. _____ Write 3 kinds of dogs and wait for a description of each.

   _____ Write 3 categories of retrievers and wait for a description of each.

2. _____ The instructor is going to describe 2 categories of dogs.

   _____ The instructor is going to mention the names of 2 breeds.

3. _____ Listen for the definition of *retriever*.

   _____ Listen for 2 differences between the 2 breeds.

4. _____ Listen for 5 differences between hunting dogs and herding dogs.

   _____ Listen for 5 more kinds of dogs; you should have a total of 7.

5. _____ Write 2 similarities between beagles and detector dogs.

   _____ Write 2 reasons most detector dogs are beagles.

6. _____ Listen for an explanation of how the 2 types of working dogs are different.

   _____ Now the instructor is going to explain how 2 breeds of dogs are used for 1 type of work.

STRATEGY

Listening for Main Ideas and Details

First, decide which style of note-taking you'd like to practice in this chapter, an outline or a concept map. After you choose, work from the general to the specific. In other words, the first time you listen to the lecture, you don't have to take notes—try to understand the general topic. Then listen again and again, trying to understand a little more each time. Go back and look at the vocabulary on page 161; did you hear any of those words in the lecture? Leave a lot of blank space in your notes so that you can fill it in later as you listen and understand more.

ACTIVITY **10** **Listening for main ideas**

Choose either the concept map or the outline format for your notes. Then listen to the lecture and fill in the main ideas. (Hint: Look at the questions below.)

Outline
Ch. 5, Notes, Canine Colleagues

- Intro.:
  - ▪
  - ▪
  - ▪
  - ▪

    1.
    2.
    3.
    4.

1.
  - ▪
  - ▪
  - ▪

2.
  - ▪
  - ▪

3.
  - ▪
  - ▪
  - ▪

4.

Concept map

Ch. 5, Notes, Canine Colleagues

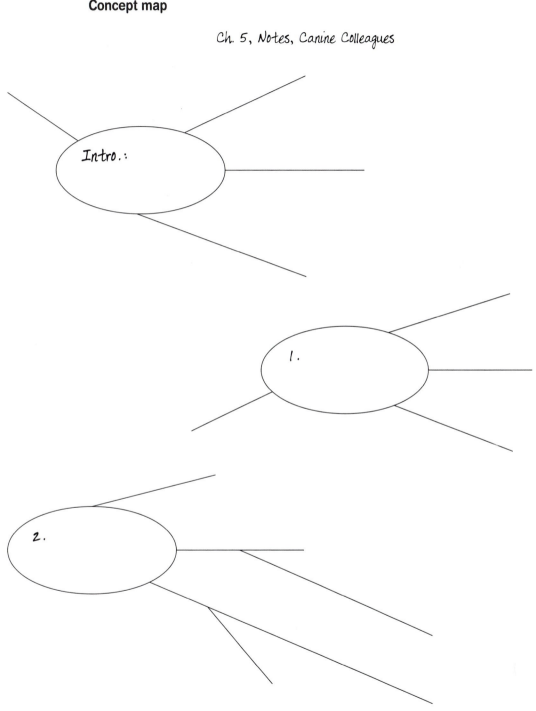

Intro.:

1.

2.

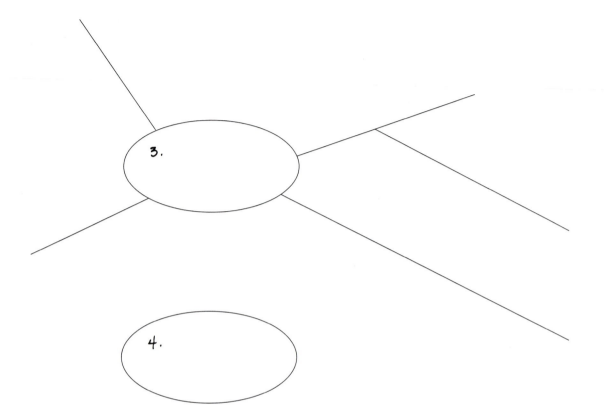

Can you answer these questions?

1. In the introduction, what does the professor say is the topic of today's lecture?
2. How many types of dogs does the professor talk about?
3. What is the name of each type?

 ACTIVITY **11** **Listening for details**

Listen to the lecture again; this time write the answers to these questions in your notes:

1. What is the job of each type of dog?
2. Who are the people that the dogs work with?
3. What breeds are used for each type of work?

Guessing Meaning from Context

In Chapter 4, we learned that when we hear a new word, we often need to guess its meaning. Let's review, or go over again, how we do this:

► by using the context, or language around the word

► by using cognates, or words that are similar in other languages (e.g., *certified* in English and *certifié* in French)

► by looking at how the word is used in the sentence (i.e., the grammar)

Let's look at an example (without a dictionary). In the lecture, the professor says, "Service dogs are trained to pick things up, retrieve, or get, objects, turn lights on and off, . . . bark to warn the person of possible danger. . ." If you don't know what *bark* means, but you understand the rest of the sentence, then you can guess. From the way the word is used, you know it's something that service dogs are trained to do. You also know that they do this in order to warn a person about something dangerous. What would you do to warn someone? Shout, or yell? Dogs can't shout, but they can bark—that's one way dogs communicate with people.

Sometimes when you try to guess the meaning of a word you hear, you have a general understanding of the word, for example, you know that it has a positive or a negative meaning, but you're not sure of the exact meaning. That's OK unless it's an important word in the lecture. In that case, look up the word in a dictionary.

ACTIVITY 12 Guessing meaning from context

Listen to the sentence from the lecture, and guess the meaning of the word(s). Circle the letter of the best choice: a, b, or c.

You hear:

Guide dogs wear a specially designed harness that the handler holds onto, and the dog guides, or leads, the handler.

Harness: **a.** a breed of dog
b. a kind of person
c. a piece of equipment (You should circle letter *c.*)

1. *paralyzed:*
   a. blind
   b. helped out
   c. unable to move

2. *wheelchair . . .*
   a. a special institution
   b. a special chair
   c. a type of disability

3. *keen:*
   a. disastrous
   b. sharp
   c. slow

4. *avalanche . . .*
   a. an event
   b. a person
   c. a sense

5. *rewarded:*
   a. given something good
   b. picked up
   c. treated badly

6. *sniff out:*
   a. destroy
   b. find by smelling
   c. leave out

Recognizing Teacher Talk

During a lecture, students listen and take notes, and when they don't understand part of what the professor is saying, they show that in their notes, for example with a question mark or two (??), so that later they can ask the professor to clarify, or make that part clear. In some classes, students ask questions while the professor is talking. In other classes, the professor waits until the end of the lecture to answer questions.

When do you raise your hand to ask a question? The professor will probably wait until the end of the lecture to indicate, or show, that it is time for questions. He or she won't give you much time to respond, so you have to be quick and raise your hand immediately.

Master Student Tip

▼ **Be an Attentive Listener**

Being an attentive listener means showing the speaker that you are listening carefully. Master students do this through body language: eye contact, facial expressions, and posture. They look at the speaker, they nod their head and respond to questions, and they sit up straight. This communicates to the speaker that they are paying attention.

Here are some expressions that the professor might use to indicate that it's time to ask your question:

Are there any questions?

Let's open the floor to questions.

Do any of you have any questions? Is all of that clear? Did you get all of that?

The professor's body language will also tell you that it's time to ask questions. He or she might raise his or her eyebrows, turn the head to the side a little, and look around the class, or make a hand gesture, for example, open the palm of the hand.

🎧 **ACTIVITY 13 Knowing when to ask questions**

Listen to the lecture again and answer these questions:

1. When does the professor in "Canine Colleagues" offer to answer questions, in the middle of the lecture or at the end?
2. What expression does the instructor use to indicate that it's time for the students to ask questions?

◤ Using Your Lecture Notes

STRATEGY

Using Note Cards

In Chapter 3, you learned how to use 3" × 5" ("three by five") cards, or note cards, for lecture notes. Another way to use these cards for studying is to use them as "flash cards." Write a question about the lecture on one side of the card, and write the answer on the other side. Then you can use the cards to quiz yourself. If you can't answer a question without looking at the back of the card, then you know that you have to study more!

Example:

one side of card

> What's the history of the dog-human relationship?

other side of card

> > 10K yrs ago, dogs + people: friends
> >   - for protection
> >   - helped w/hunting + herding

ACTIVITY 14 **Using note cards**

Look at your lecture notes and write one question on one side of a note card.

Write the answer to the question, in note form, on the back of the card.

Do this five times.

Close your book and notebook. With a partner, take turns asking and answering each other's questions.

Part 2

▽ Looking at Language

STRATEGY

Pronunciation: Intonation of Questions

The most important feature in the pronunciation of questions in English is intonation. In the following examples, the intonation is shown by the arrows. Intonation, or change in tone, makes a language sound like singing because your voice goes up and down as you talk, very much like the change in tones in music (*do, re, mi, fa, so, la, ti, do*). When you ask an information question (*what, where, how, . . .*), your voice goes **down** at the end, but when you ask a yes/no question, your voice goes **up** at the end. Listen to the intonation as your instructor reads these questions:

🎧 **Present Tense**

1. *What is the difference between x and y?* ↘
2. *Do you **mean** that x and y have the **same** characteristics?* ↗
3. *What breeds do they use for guide dogs?* ↘

Past Tense

1. *What was the difference between x and y?* ↘
2. *Did you **mean** that x and y had the **same** characteristics?* ↗
3. *What breeds did they use for guide dogs?* ↘

When you ask about the past, you usually use *did* in the question. When you make a request, you use *could* or *would* in the question. Look at these examples of requests:

🎧 **Request (You're Asking for Something)**

    *Could **I have** one of the **papers** you **handed out?*** ↗
    *(Could **you give** me one of the **papers** you **handed out?**)* ↗
    *Would **you** re**peat** the **part** about archaeologists?* ↗

Grammar: Past-Tense Questions

Past-tense questions follow the same pattern as present-tense questions. Only one word in the question changes—and that word tells the listener if the question is about the past or present. It's a function word—not a content word—so in your pronunciation it's not stressed. Look at the examples above, and circle the word that shows the tense.

ACTIVITY 15 **Correcting errors**

Correct the errors in the following past-tense questions, and practice saying the correct version aloud.

Example: What ~~he said~~, *archaeologists* or *anthropologists?*

What did he say, archaeologists or anthropologists?

1. Where the instructor said she put the grades?

2. When he say was the last day?

3. What do you said about the quiz?

4. What did she said about the assignment?

5. When she said no make-ups, what she meant?

6. Did he said the homework was due tomorrow?

7. You can tell us about the midterm exam?

8. I can have one, please?

ACTIVITY **16** **Listening for intonation and sentence stress**

Listen to the following and put a check mark (✔) beside the sentence you hear.

Example: (You will hear only the intonation—not the words.)

_____ Did she say how many pages?

___✓___ How many pages does she want?

1. _____ Were you in the lab today?

   _____ When did you go to the lab?

2. _____ Did he say the paper was due this week?

   _____ What did he say about the assignment?

3. _____ Sorry. Could you say that again?

   _____ I'm sorry. I didn't hear you.

4. _____ Did you say the midterm was tomorrow?

   _____ What was the date of the midterm exam?

5. _____ Did classes start in August?

   _____ When did classes start this year?

6. _____ Would you please repeat that?

   _____ Repeat the last part, please.

7. _____ Is he serious?

   _____ Tell me he's kidding.

ACTIVITY 17   **Practicing intonation and sentence stress**

Work with a partner to practice pronouncing the questions in the previous activity. Then repeat, but instead of reading the sentences, hum[1] them.

◸ Academic Speaking Task 1

Asking Questions for Clarification

If you don't understand part of a lecture, don't be afraid to ask the professor to clarify, or make clear, what he or she said. Many times other students have the same question, so you will not only be helping yourself, but you will help clarify the information for your classmates, too. It's your responsibility as a student to make sure that you understand, and it's the instructor's responsibility to help you understand. If you have more questions, you can see the instructor during her or his office hours. You can find the professor's office hours in the course syllabus.

Nonverbal Communication: Asking Questions

Remember the importance of nonverbal communication, or body language, when you want to ask a question in class. You need to use eye contact—look directly at the professor to get her or his attention. In most large classes, you should also raise your hand and wait until the professor calls on you.

ACTIVITY 18   **Asking questions for clarification**

Unscramble the following words to make a question.

> **Example:** about / did / dog / fourth / of / say / she / the / type / What / ?
>
> *What did she say about the fourth type of dog?*

1. and / beginning / call / did / dogs / humans / In / lecture / of / the / the / what / you / ?

---

1. *hum* = sing without words with your mouth closed

2. ago / beings / did / dogs / How / human / live / many / with / years / ?

3. 11 / about / did / say / September / What / you / ?

4. and / breeds / do / dogs / for / rescue / search / they / use / What / ?

5. DEA / did / for / stand / What / ?

6. about / again / Could / detector / dogs / explain / part / the / you / ?

7. a / and / did / *feathered* / legs / mean / said / tail / what / When / you / you / ?

8. assistance / did / dogs / for / name / other / use / What / you / ?

9. about / I'm / part / repeat / retrievers / sorry / the / the / two / would / you / ?

10. beagles / detector / Did / dogs / for / say / they / use / you / ?

ACTIVITY 19 Role-playing

Choose one person from your group to play the role of the instructor. Looking at your notes, ask "your instructor" questions from the previous activity or any other questions about the lecture, "Canine Colleagues."

◤ Academic Speaking Task 2

Preparing a Short Presentation

In Chapter 4, you practiced three important presentation skills: eye contact, posture, and voice quality. In this chapter, you will continue to practice these skills, and you will prepare and practice a three-minute speech. In order to plan what you are going to say, look at the topics in Activity 20. Then follow these steps:

Steps in Preparing a Speech

1. Choose a topic that you are interested in and know something about.
2. Think about the topic and take notes.
3. Organize your notes so that there is a beginning, a middle, and an end.
4. Practice your speech in front of someone or in front of a mirror, timing yourself so that it's at least three minutes long.
5. Make any changes that you think are necessary.

Do's and Don'ts

1. Use your notes to help you remember the information, but don't read from a script you've written! Remember how important it is to look at your audience.

   Example of notes, which should fit on a 3" × 5" card:

   > - what I've learned frm dogs: responsibility, discipline, & loyalty
   > - my family + dogs: Mitsy, Caesar, + Taffy (on board + pix of breeds)
   > - lrned respnsb'ty thru taking care of dogs: ex.s ("vet" on board)
   > - lrnd discipline thru training: "housetrain"(on board) + teach basic commands: ex.s
   > - not easy -- takes time, repetition, & patience
   > - lrned importnce of loyalty: my dogs were my friends: always . . .
   > - bec. they were loyal, I am now loyal to my friends
   > - Mitsy, Caesar, + Taffy, even tho dogs, were important part of my life

2. Don't memorize something that you've written in paragraph form—it will sound artificial. You want it to sound as natural as possible. This is easy if you choose a topic that you're familiar with. The only kind of writing you do should be in note form.

3. Don't assume[2] that your audience knows anything about your topic. Explain everything and use simple language that your classmates will understand.

4. Explain all vocabulary that you think your audience does not know: Write it on the board, a transparency, or a handout. For example, if you had to use your dictionary to look up a word, then you probably need to explain that word to your classmates.

5. Use visuals, if possible, to help your audience understand. Draw a picture, bring a photograph, use Power Point, or bring something to show your audience. Make sure it's big enough for everyone to see.

6. Speak clearly, stressing the content words.

7. Don't rush—take your time, relax, and enjoy yourself!

Your instructor will show you an example of a three-minute speech following the steps and the Do's and Don'ts from above.

ACTIVITY 20 Planning a presentation

Look at the following topics and choose one for a three-minute speech.

Follow the steps above to prepare for your presentation.

Write your final notes on a 3" × 5" card.

Choose from these topics:

a. Talk about your personal experience with animals and/or pets.
b. Discuss your family's attitude toward animals.
c. Compare dogs and cats (or two other kinds of animals you are familiar with).
d. Talk about an animal you are afraid of.
e. Tell a story about a famous animal from a book, movie, television, or the news (fiction or nonfiction).
f. Describe a dog breed that you know about, or compare two breeds.
g. Explain how animals are used as symbols in literature, films, or advertising.

2. *assume* = think sthg. is true

Master Student Tip

Never Give Up!

When speaking to a group of students, Sir Winston Churchill, famous statesman and British prime minister during World War II, said, "Never give up, never give up." *Give up* means *to yield*, or say, "I lose; you win; I'll stop fighting now." Master students know that in order to succeed they can never give up. It's important to work hard and be persistent.

ACTIVITY 21 **Practicing your speech**

Use your notes from Activity 20 to practice your speech.

1. Sit facing a classmate.

   Student A: Give your three-minute speech.
   Student B: Listen and take notes. If something is not clear, ask a question.

2. Move to another desk and practice with a different partner. Make any changes to your speech that you or your partner(s) think are necessary.

3. When you feel comfortable giving your speech, volunteer to speak in front of the entire class.

Part 3

ASSESSING YOUR LISTENING AND SPEAKING SKILLS

▷ **Getting Ready for the Test: Self-Assessment**

ACTIVITY 22 **Evaluating your skills**

Evaluate yourself on the following skills by putting a check mark (✔) in the column that best describes how you feel you can do each. For every check mark in the third column, go back and practice before you take the test.

Listening I can:	Great	OK	Need to practice
1. understand some common phrasal verbs			
2. guess the meanings of words from the context			
3. understand & use new vocabulary			
4. listen for main ideas & details			
5. recognize signal words			
6. know when to ask questions in a lecture			
7. distinguish between rising & falling intonation			

Speaking I am able to:	Great	OK	Need to practice
1. talk about the relationship between dogs & people, especially three types of working dogs			
2. use some separable phrasal verbs correctly			
3. use my dictionary for pronunciation			
4. ask questions for clarification			
5. ask questions with correct grammar, word stress, & intonation			
6. give a short oral presentation			
Study skills I should:			
1. distinguish between objective & subjective statements			
2. listen to an animal science lecture & take notes			
3. be an attentive listener			
4. be persistent & never give up			
5. use note cards as flash cards			
6. plan a short oral presentation			

▷ Chapter Test

In order to evaluate your progress, your instructor may ask you to do some or all of the following activities for the chapter test.

Listening Test Activities

ACTIVITY 23 Note-taking

Listen to the following mini-lecture and take notes, using abbreviations and symbols. Write your notes on a separate sheet of paper that you will hand in later.

ACTIVITY 24 Understanding phrasal verbs

Listen to the sentences and check (✓) the idea that is closest in meaning to what you hear.

You hear:

The assignment is due on Wednesday.

You check:

_____✓_____ Hand in your homework Wednesday.

_____ Look up *assignment* by Wednesday.

1. _____ Detector dogs assist in national disasters.

   _____ Detector dogs help out government organizations.

2. _____ Please put away your identification.

   _____ Please take out your identification.

3. _____ You forgot to do the evaluation.

   _____ You left the administration, which is OK.

4. _____ When did you hear?

   _____ When did you fill it out?

5. _____ Please turn on the air conditioning.

   _____ Please take off the air conditioning.

ACTIVITY 25 **Using your notes**

Using your notes from the mini-lecture in Part A, listen to the questions and circle the letter of the best answer.

1. **a.** Detector dogs working for government agencies.

   b. Snoopy and the comic strip, "Peanuts."

   c. The people who work for the USDA and DEA.

   d. Prohibited agricultural products in the U.S.

2. **a.** Beagles.

   b. Brigades.

   c. Peanuts.

   d. Scent dogs.

3. **a.** Because they work like soldiers.

   b. Because of their great sense of smell.

   c. Because of their temperament.

   d. Because they like to be rewarded.

4. **a.** In the United States capital.

   b. At the USDA in Washington.

   c. At international airports.

   d. In Mexico.

5. **a.** To protect the USDA and the DEA.

   b. To detect banned substances.

   c. To find explosives using their excellent eyesight.

   d. To attack the enemy like soldiers.

6. **a.** 131

   b. 75,000

   c. 5,000,000

   d. 220,000,000

7. **a.** Dogs.

   b. Humans.

   c. Neither—they both have the same number.

   d. Yes, they do.

8. **a.** To sniff out drugs.

   b. To detect explosives.

   c. To protect the DEA building.

   d. To find prohibited agriculture.

9. **a.** They bark.

   b. They carry the item to the handler.

   c. They sit next to the item.

   d. They eat the item.

10. **a.** The Dog Employment Agency.

   b. The Department of Emergency Agriculture.

   c. The Detectors for Enforcement and Agriculture.

   d. The Drug Enforcement Agency.

Speaking Test Activities

ACTIVITY 26 **Asking questions for clarification**

Look at your notes from the mini-lecture, Activity 23, and ask three questions.

ACTIVITY 27 **Talking about the lecture**

Answer questions and talk about the lecture, "Canine Colleagues," or the mini-lecture, "Beagle Brigade." Your instructor may allow you to use your notes.

ACTIVITY 28 **Understanding and using phrasal verbs**

Answer the questions that your instructor asks you.

ACTIVITY 29 **Distinguishing between fact and opinion**

Listen to the sentence that your instructor reads to you. Explain why it is either a statement of fact or opinion.

Speaking Evaluation Checklist

Your instructor may use the following checklists to assess your speaking in class activities and/or in the Speaking Test.

Speaking evaluation	OK	Needs work	Example(s)
Listening			
► understood question			
Content			
► answered correctly			
Language use			
► expressed ideas clearly			
► used language from chapter			
Pronunciation			
► clear & comprehensible			
► not too fast or slow			
► loud enough			
Nonverbal communication			
► appropriate eye contact			
► correct posture			

Oral presentation	OK	Needs work	Example(s)
Preparation			
➤ organized ideas			
➤ used notes effectively			
➤ explained new vocabulary			
➤ answered audience questions			
Language use			
➤ expressed ideas clearly			
➤ spoke naturally			
Pronunciation			
➤ comprehensible			
➤ not too fast or slow			
➤ loud enough			
Nonverbal communication			
➤ appropriate eye contact			
➤ correct posture & gestures			
➤ effective visuals			

WEB POWER

You will find additional exercises related to the content in this chapter at **http://esl.college.hmco.com/esl**.

Amazing
Mice

ACADEMIC FOCUS:
BEHAVIORAL SCIENCES ▶ PSYCHOLOGY

Academic Listening and Speaking Objectives

In this chapter, you will work individually, in pairs, and in small groups to:

▶ Learn about the scientific method in a psychology experiment
▶ Come to a conclusion using inductive or deductive reasoning
▶ Review abbreviations and symbols from past chapters
▶ Understand and use more common phrasal verbs
▶ Learn to become a critical listener
▶ Express similarities and differences using *as . . . as*
▶ Interpret a line graph
▶ Use the simple past tense with correct pronunciation
▶ Talk with your professor about a problem
▶ Plan and give a short oral presentation

Part 1

EFFECTIVE ACADEMIC LISTENING

Psychology is one of the most popular general education courses on college campuses. The lecture in this chapter, "Amazing Mice," is about the experimental method as it is used in psychology.

▷ Getting Ready for the Lecture

To understand the lecture better, read the following selection to learn how psychologists and other scientists think about research.

PSYCHOLOGISTS AS SCIENTISTS

1   The field of psychology is wide-ranging, which means people trained as psychologists may work in a variety of settings. For example, school psychologists work in education, industrial psychologists work for businesses, and forensic psychologists work with the police and the legal system. Although they work in different areas, all these psychologists depend on their colleagues who work as researchers to give them more information about what is going on in the field of psychology.

2   Research psychology is a science, which, according to one dictionary, means it depends on the "observation, study, and theoretical explanation of natural events."* That definition may sound simple, but it is actually very complex. It is complex because of what is *not* expressed, but understood. It is understood that all scientists approach their work in a certain way and that they follow certain rules. This is fundamental to scientific research.

*The American Heritage ESL Dictionary. (1998). Boston: Houghton Mifflin.

3   Scientists approach their work objectively, sharing certain assumptions and unwritten rules. One assumption is that they work systematically. That means they conduct their research very carefully, making observations and precise measurements and avoiding all possible errors.

4   A second assumption is that scientists are unbiased and ethical. In other words, they treat everyone and everything the same way, and they do what is morally right. No one person or thing gets better or worse treatment than the others, and everyone in a research study, including an animal, is treated humanely. Being ethical also means that the scientists will not be influenced by anything outside their research, such as someone interested in their work who might want to offer them money or gifts.

5   A third assumption is that, when possible, scientists quantify their results. They use numbers in the form of graphs, charts, tables, and statistics. In addition, scientists believe that their research is successful if other scientists can duplicate it (and come up with similar results). And last, scientists are skeptical. They don't automatically assume that their conclusions are the only explanations for whatever they are studying; they constantly doubt and ask more questions.

6   As scientists, psychologists study mental processes and behavior. As researchers, they use different methods to describe and predict behavior and mental processes: naturalistic observation, case studies, and surveys. Psychologists also use experiments to determine causes and/or effects of behavior and thinking.

ACTIVITY **1**   **Making inferences**

Whenever you read, you make inferences, or conclusions, from the information. To be a good reader in college, you need to think logically and make the right inferences. Practice making the right inferences by doing the following:

1. Read the statement.
2. If you can infer, or conclude, the information in the statement from the reading, write a plus sign (+) in the blank. If not, write a minus sign (−).
3. Compare your answers with your classmates' and explain how you came to your conclusions.

Example:

___−___ A psychology researcher would consider using friends and family members to participate in a survey.

Explanation:

This would not be an objective study. Friends and family might give answers they think the researcher wants to hear. That would influence the results; it would also be biased.

1. _____ There are more research psychologists than forensic psychologists.

2. _____ Research psychologists depend on school psychologists to help them when doing educational research.

3. _____ Research psychology is not a real science.

4. _____ Scientists observe events and try to explain them through theories.

5. _____ If an instructor treats one student differently from the others, he or she is being biased.

6. _____ Stealing is considered ethical behavior.

7. _____ *Systematic* probably means "careful."

8. _____ Psychologists use four types of research.

9. _____ If two scientists conduct the same research and come up with different results, there's a problem.

10. _____ A psychologist might study why some students cheat during exams.

STRATEGY

Using Logical Thinking

In the previous activity, you had to infer, or make conclusions, from information that was given to you. That means you used logical thinking, or reasoning. Whenever we make conclusions, we use either deductive or inductive reasoning.

Deductive reasoning works from the general to the specific. It often uses rules, definitions, or facts (general) to make a conclusion about a specific case or individual. The conclusion is true only if the general statement is true. Look at this example:

General rule	⟶	Specific conclusion
Good researchers have to be careful and systematic. (fact)		Researcher X is not careful, so she is **not** a good researcher.

When using **inductive** reasoning, you make conclusions from the specific to the general. Researchers observe the behavior of a small number of people, for example, and in their conclusions they make generalizations and predictions about all people. The conclusion is not true if you can think of just one counterexample—that is, an example showing the statement is false. The lecture from this chapter uses inductive reasoning:

Specific case	⟶	General conclusion
An experiment with twenty mice shows that alcohol has a negative effect on their ability to learn to get through a maze.		Alcohol has a negative effect on learning.

It is not possible to be absolutely sure, so the inductive conclusion usually includes words such as *may*, *might*, and *could*, and phrases such as *It appears that*, *It seems that*, and *Results suggest that* . . .

ACTIVITY 2 Identifying logical thinking

Work with a group to fill in the table below.

1. *Identify the reasoning (inductive or deductive) in each of the following situations listed on the next page.*
2. *Decide whether the conclusion is logical or illogical.*
3. *Give reasons for both.*

Example: The product of two negative numbers is always a positive number, so if *x* is a negative number and *y* is a positive number, *xy* is positive.

Situation	D (Deductive) or I (Inductive) + Reason	Logical or Illogical Conclusion + Reason
Example	D: starts w/ gen'l rule + goes on to specific ex.	Illog.: rule says 2 neg. #s. The ex. has a positive #.
1		
2		
3		
4		
5		

1. Professor Allen gave me a C– in his English comp class. Two of my friends failed his class, and other students told me they didn't pass, either. On the list of final grades outside his office there are always a lot of Ds and Fs. I would conclude that Professor Allen is most likely a tough grader.

2. I don't get along with Sam, Sue, or Steve, who are all friends. I haven't met their friend Scott, yet, but I'm sure that because he is a friend of theirs, I will not like him, either.

3. At the University of California, Berkeley, almost half of the new freshmen are Asian American. Conclusion: Asians must be more intelligent than other ethnic groups.

4. All instructors are wonderful. _____ is an instructor. Therefore, he or she is wonderful.

5. You notice that the sum of two negative numbers is always another negative number, so if x is a negative number and y is a negative number, $(x + y)$ is negative.

POWER GRAMMAR

Phrasal Verbs

As you saw in Chapter 5, phrasal verbs are common in more conversational English. Professors often use this informal, spoken language in their lectures in order to make the information easier for students to understand.

Phrasal verbs are verbs that consist of two or more words, for example, *go on*. The first word is a verb (*go*), and the second word is a preposition (*on*). The words function as a whole, or phrase, and have a different meaning from their separate parts. The following phrasal verbs are **in**separable, which means the verb and preposition are never separated. Some common phrasal verbs and their meanings are listed below:

Phrasal Verb Meaning

go on	happen; continue
come up with	propose or produce an idea
get back to	return
go over	examine, review (sthg.)

Work with a partner to match the following definitions with these phrasal verbs:

clock in	*get along (with)*	*get through*	*get up*
make it through	*run out (of)*	*stand for*	*keep on*
stand out	*wear off*		

1. arise from bed
2. be distinctive or prominent; attract attention

(Continued)

3. be slowly reduced in effect, e.g., lipstick
4. be successful in a difficult situation
5. continue (doing sthg.)
6. finish (sthg.); complete (sthg.)
7. have a friendly relationship
8. represent
9. use all the supply of sthg.
10. swipe your ID card when you begin to work

Pronunciation: Word Stress

Most phrasal verbs are stressed on the preposition, or the second word in the phrase (exception: *stand for*). This contrasts with the pronunciation of the noun form, which is stressed on the first word in the phrase and often has a different meaning from the verb.

Examples:

Verb	Meaning	Noun	Meaning
make **UP**	redo, retake (a quiz, for ex.); form, constitute.	**MAKE**-up	cosmetics for the skin
take **OFF**	remove (clothing, for ex.)	**TAKE**-off	airplane time of flight
try **OUT**	test or use sthg. experimentally; take a qualifying test as for drama or music	**TRY**-out	audition; test to find out qualifications of applicants

Because phrasal verbs are content words, they are usually stressed in sentences. Look at these examples (the stressed syllables are in **bold** print):

> I *missed* a *quiz* last *week*.
> The *teach*er said I *can't* make it *up*.

ACTIVITY 3 **Unscrambling phrasal verbs**

Unscramble the following words to make a complete sentence. (Be careful: one phrasal verb is separable!) With a partner, practice saying each using the correct sentence stress.

> **Example:** along / doesn't / get / her / She / supervisor. / with
>
> *She doesn't get along with her supervisor.*

1. American / APA / Association. / for / Psychological / stands / the

2. drug / find / goal / how / is / it / long / of / off. / out / study / takes / the / The / the / to / to / wear

3. a / all / but / it / It / long / made / maze. / mice / the / the / through / time / took

4. at / certain / data / look / numbers / out. / researchers / stand / their / usually / When

5. a / can / faster / figure / maze / mice / mice. / out / Rested / than / tired

6. but / going / more / of / out / psychologist / ran / she / talk / The / time. / to / was

7. a / a / Bosnian / came / for / great / idea / up / student / survey. / The / with

8. data / fired. / he / He / important / left / out / so / some / was

9. back / get / going / Let's / on? / to / What's / work. (2 sentences)

10. come / conclusions. / hope / others / Researchers / similar / that / up/ will / with

ACTIVITY 4 **Understanding phrasal verbs**

Listen to the following sentences and check (✓) the idea that is closest in meaning to what you hear.

You hear:

How long has this been going on?

You check:

_____ How long has this been finished?

___✓___ How long has this been happening?

1. _____ Some psychologists have certain characteristics like sociologists.
   _____ Some psychologists study people's personalities.

2. _____ Successful people keep on trying.

   _____ Successful people sometimes fail, but they are able to hide it well.

3. _____ Good students prepare for their exams the night beforehand.
   _____ Good students study every day.

4. _____ Psychologists are always coming up with different research studies.
   _____ Psychologists never get through their research studies when they need to.

5. _____ Drivers using cell phones are not as attentive to the road as drivers without cell phones.
   _____ Drivers using hand-held cell phones are as inattentive to their driving as drivers with headsets.

6. _____ People who are drunk receive negative effects from alcohol.

   _____ People who are drunk need time to get sober.*

*sober = not intoxicated or affected by the use of alcoholic beverages or drugs

STRATEGY

Becoming a Critical Listener

As educated adults, we should be critical thinkers and listeners. That means we think about what we read or hear, and we evaluate it before accepting or rejecting it. In order to evaluate information, we consider who says it (the source) and how reasonable it is. We can apply critical thinking by asking ourselves these questions when we read or hear something:

1. What am I being asked to believe or accept?
2. Who is the person giving me the information, and what are her or his motives?
3. What evidence is given as support?
4. Are there other ways to interpret the evidence?
5. What conclusions are most reasonable?

Let's look at an example from television. You see an advertisement for a computer school where you can get a degree and find a job in six months. A well-dressed, good-looking young woman says that she graduated from the school and is now a successful professional working with computers.

1. What am I being asked to believe or accept?

You're asked to believe that if you go to that school, you can get a degree in computers, find a good job, and be like the woman in the ad—all in six months.

2. Who is the person giving me the information, and what are her or his motives?

The school is giving you the information; it needs students in order to stay in business. The young woman could be a graduate of the school, or she could be an actor. In either case, she was paid to make the commercial.

3. What evidence is given as support?

The word of the young woman is given as support. This is called a testimonial.

(Continued)

4. Are there other ways to interpret the evidence?

Yes, because of the information that is **not** given in the ad. You need more information to make a judgment about this school: Is it accredited? What is the school's reputation? What kind of certificate does it offer in six months?

5. What conclusions are most reasonable?

The ad may be very attractive, but be careful. A good school meets certain standards by being "accredited" by a professional organization. Accreditation means that the school follows the same rules as other academic institutions. It means that the instructors all have the required degree (bachelor's, master's, or doctorate) and full-time contracts, and the classes are of high quality.

You should get more information about this school before believing the TV ad.

ACTIVITY 5 Being a critical listener

1. Listen to the following radio broadcasts and take notes.
2. Work with a group and decide if the broadcast is an ad (advertisement) or a news report. Then answer the five critical-thinking questions above.
3. Report your answers to the class.

STRATEGY

Words from the Lecture

In order to understand the lecture in this chapter, "Amazing Mice," you need to know the meanings of the words in the following activity. Many of these words are found on the Academic Word List (AWL), which means they are used frequently in a variety of academic texts. In other words, you are going to see and hear these AWL words in your other classes—no matter what your major—so you should know them.

In the list that follows, definitions are from *The American Heritage English as a Second Language Dictionary*, 1998, Houghton Mifflin Company. The abbreviation ***sthg.*** is used for *something*, ***sbdy.*** for *somebody*, and ***esp.*** for *especially*.

approach A way or method of dealing or working with sbdy./ sthg.

assumption The act of assuming or supposing (considering that sthg. is true, real, or sure to happen).

basis A foundation on which sthg. rests.

bias A prejudice.

data **1.** Information, esp. when it is to be analyzed or used as the basis for a decision. **2.** Information, usually in numerical form, suitable for processing by computer.

duplicate **1.** To make an exact copy of (sthg.); *duplicate a key*.

2. To do or perform (sthg.) again; repeat: *duplicate an experiment*.

factors Things that help cause a certain result; elements or ingredients: *Many factors contributed to the success of the celebration*.

logical Using or agreeing with the principles of logic, or reasoning.

maze A complicated and confusing network of paths.

overall **1.** Including everything; total: *the overall cost of the project*. **2.** Viewed as a whole; general: *the overall effect created by the new furniture*.

range An extent or amount of difference: *a price range*.

sequence **1.** A following of one thing after another; succession: *the sequence of events*. **2.** The order in which things or events occur or are arranged: *I followed the sequence of steps outlined in the book*.

ACTIVITY 6 **Expanding your vocabulary**

Fill in the blank with the correct word from the list. Look at #1 as an example.

1. Psychologists work in a wide ____range____ of professional positions, from testing school children to conducting research for industries.

2. When doing experiments on learning, psychologists have to take many _____ into consideration, for example a person's age, gender, and socioeconomic background.

3. I don't think I'm going to pass my physics class, but _____, I'm doing OK this semester.

4. The biological _____ to psychology emphasizes biological causes of behavior, whereas the cognitive _____ emphasizes how people process information.

5. One _____ that is made about researchers is that they are ethical in all aspects of their work.

6. A _____ is not used just for small animals, such as mice. It can also be large enough for humans. For example, some English gardens are designed so that people have a hard time finding their way from one end to another.

7. One test of inductive reasoning asks you to look at a _____ of numbers, such as 5, 6, 8, 11, . . . , find a pattern, and predict the next numbers.

8. Researchers also try to find patterns when looking at _____ that they collect in their studies.

9. Objective observation is the _____ for scientific research.

10. If–then statements form the basis for deductive reasoning, or thinking. For example, if $a = b$, and $c = a$, then a _____ conclusion is that $c = b$.

11. _____ is subjective because it indicates a personal preference. That is why it has no place in the objective world of science.

12. If you _____ someone else's work, it's not considered cheating because you give the person credit for her or his work.

13. If you want a donkey to move, you can use either a carrot or a stick _____. Use the carrot as a reward—something positive—if the donkey is cooperative, or use a stick—something negative—if the donkey refuses.

ACTIVITY   7   Practicing word stress

Work with a partner to practice hearing and pronouncing the stress of these AWL words that appear in the lecture.

1. *Choose one of the words and say it aloud.*
2. *Tell your partner if the stress pattern he or she hears is correct or not.*
3. *Do the odd or even numbers, and then switch.*

   Example: *range*

[1-1]	[2-1]
range	ranges
ranged	ranging

   Student A: *Ranged.*
   Student B: *2-1. (Two one)*
   Student A: *No. I'll say it again: ranged.*
   Student B: *1-1 (One one)*
   Student A: *Right.*

Remember to tap out the syllables with your fingers, or use some other physical movement to feel the syllables and stress.

1. *sequence*

[2-1]	[3-1]	[3-2]	[4-2]
sequence sequenced	sequences sequencing	sequential	sequentially

2. *logical*

[2-1]	[3-1]	[3-2]	[4-2]
logic	logical logically	logician logicians	illogical illogically

3. *factor*

[2-1]	[3-1]
factor	factoring
factors	
factored	

4. *assumption*

[2-2]	[3-2]
assume	assuming
assumes	assumption
assumed	assumptions

5. *approach*

[2-2]	[3-2]	[4-2]	[5-3]
approach approached	approaches approaching	approachable	unapproachable

ACTIVITY **8**   **Using academic words**

Ask the questions in Appendix 1 on page 237 as your partner scans Activity 7 for the correct words to use in the answers. Do the first four and then switch.

Example:

Student A (on page 237): *How did you deal with the problem— objectively or subjectively?*

Student B (above): *I **approached** it objectively.* or
*I **approached** it subjectively.*

▽ Getting Information from the Lecture

STRATEGY

Reviewing Abbreviations and Symbols

Good note-takers listen attentively and use their own system of abbreviations and symbols. Here are some abbreviations and symbols from previous chapters. See how many you remember by matching them with the words they represent.

@ bec cuz e.g. esp. grp int'l lrng nat'l ♀

psych rsrch # no w/ w/o ♂ ✦ ↓ → =

Word/Idea You Hear	Symbol/Abbreviation You Write
especially	esp.
research	
psychology	
male(s), men, boy(s)	
female(s), women, girl(s)	
number	
with	
without	
at	
learning	
group	
decrease, low, lower, …	
cause(s), results in, …	
because	
plus, and, in addition, positive	
for example, an example of this	
is/are (be), means, is the same as, equals …	

ACTIVITY **9** **Using abbreviations and symbols**

Listen to parts of the lecture and complete the following notes by writing abbreviations and/or symbols. Feel free to use your own.

You hear:

This week we're going to study research methods in psychology ...

You write:

this wk: study ___rsch___ methods in psych.

1. Today: look @ _____ of scientf. mthd used in _____

2. Why study scientf. mthd? _____ basis of how we think, make

   judgmnts, do business in acad. _____ scientf. wrld

3. in science: conduct exprmts on animals before people—in psych:

   _____ looking @ _____, use mice to see how fast they figure

   out maze

4. 2 _____ of mice: 1 _____ alcohol (control _____) +

   1 _____ alcohol (experimtl _____)

5. make sure same _____ of _____ in each grp + similar
   range of ages

STRATEGY

Being an Independent Note-taker

In this chapter, you will practice the note-taking strategies from previous chapters. You need to develop your own system for taking notes that is easy for you to remember. Use a concept map, an outline, or whatever else is successful for you. Some strategies follow:

1. Use symbols and abbreviations.
2. Pay close attention.
3. Listen for main ideas and details.
4. Try to organize the ideas.
5. Leave a space where you missed information.
6. Listen for signal words.
7. Make your notes visual.
8. Ask questions for clarification.

Note-taking is a skill, like typing or playing the piano. Don't be discouraged if you're not good at it right away. The only way you can get better is by practicing; as the saying goes, "Practice makes perfect."

ACTIVITY **10** **Taking notes on your own**

Choose either the concept map or the outline format for your notes. Then listen to the lecture several times and take notes.

Ch. 6, Notes, Amazing Mice

Part 2

▽ Looking at Language

POWER GRAMMAR

As ... As

When comparing two things in English, you can use the comparative form (*more ... than, better than, less ... than*) or an expression of equality (*as ... as*). *As ... as* is used to indicate that two things are the same, or equal. It is used in the negative form (*not*) to show that one is **less** than the other. Let's look at an example:

Speed:

Mouse X	Mouse Y	Mouse Z
2 minutes (fast)	2 minutes (fast)	3.5 minutes (slow)

Less (<)	The same (=)	More (>)
Z isn't as fast as X and Y. *Z doesn't run as fast as X and Y.*	*X is as fast as Y.* *X runs as fast as Y.*	*X and Y are faster than Z.* *X and Y run faster than Z.*
	It takes X as much time as Y to get through the maze. It takes X as many minutes as Y to get through the maze.	*Z is slower than X and Y.*

Note: *As much ... as* is used with singular, uncountable nouns (*time*), and *as many ... as* is used with plural count nouns (*minutes*).

(Continued)

Pronunciation: Sentence Stress

Because comparative forms and expressions of equality are grammatical, they are function words, which means they are **not** stressed in pronunciation. Notice the content words that are stressed, or pronounced a little louder and longer than the function words:

*Z isn't as **fast** as Y.*	*X is as **fast** as Y.*	*X and Y are **faster** than Z.*
*Z doesn't **run** as **fast** as **X** and **Y**.*	*It **takes** X as **much time** as Y to get **through** the **maze.***	*X and Y run **faster** than Z.*
	*It **takes** X as **many** minutes as Y to get **through** the **maze.***	*Z is **slower** than X and Y.*

ACTIVITY 11 Using *as . . . as*

Listen to your partner read from Appendix 1, and give the equivalent, using an expression of equality (as . . . as).

Example:

Student A (on page 238): *Natasha studies a little. Kim studies a lot.*

Student B (book closed): *Natasha doesn't study as much as Kim.*

✓ Academic Speaking Task 1

Interpreting a Graph

In many college classes, graphs are used to show numerical information visually. One kind of graph that shows the relationship between two numbers is called a line graph. A line graph is often used to show differences over time. It uses a horizontal line, the *x-axis*, to show one number, and a vertical line, the *y-axis*, to show the second number. When you plot the two numbers by putting a point where the two meet, or *intersect*, you can see the relationship between that point and others. For example, in the lecture, the professor describes an experiment with mice going through a maze. Each group of mice has two numbers: an average speed for completing the maze and the number of attempts, or tries. If you plot these numbers on a graph, you can see the difference between the two groups of mice. Here are the data:

Group One

Attempt	First	Second	Third	Fourth
Average speed	5.3 min.	4.8 min.	4.2 min.	3.7 min.

Group Two

Attempt	First	Second	Third	Fourth
Average speed	6.9 min.	7.2 min.	7.4 min.	7.7 min.

Effects of Alcohol on Learning

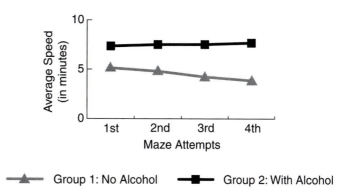

When you describe a graph like this, you should work from the general to the specific and imagine that the person you are talking with cannot see the graph. Start by saying what the graph shows (see if there's a title, or heading) and what each axis represents. Then describe the general pattern (Do the numbers increase? Decrease? What does that mean?) of each set of points and compare the two sets. If a number stands out from the others, mention it. Then, if you can, make a conclusion about what the numbers show.

Example:

This graph compares two groups of mice. The y-axis shows the groups' average speed, and the x-axis shows four attempts through a maze. Overall, the second group is not as fast as the first. In fact, its average speed is slower and slower on each attempt. Group One, on the other hand, is quicker and gets faster and faster on each attempt. It appears that the second group is not as smart as the first.

ACTIVITY 12 Interpreting a graph

Look at these graphs, and work with a partner to interpret the information. Then share with the rest of the class.

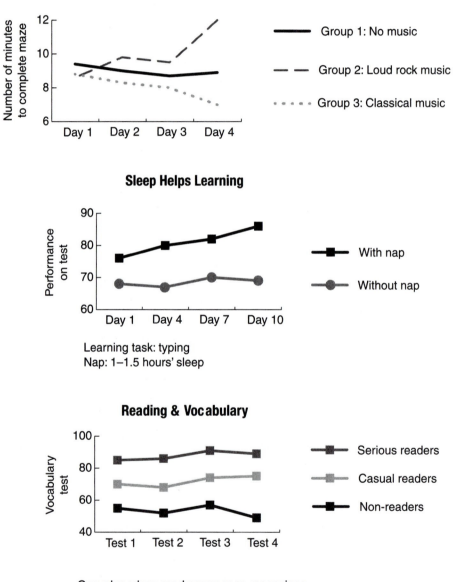

Mice, Music, & Maze

Number of minutes to complete maze

— Group 1: No music

– – Group 2: Loud rock music

· · · · Group 3: Classical music

Sleep Helps Learning

Performance on test

■ With nap

● Without nap

Learning task: typing
Nap: 1–1.5 hours' sleep

Reading & Vocabulary

Vocabulary test

■ Serious readers

■ Casual readers

■ Non-readers

Casual readers: read newspaper, magazines
Serious readers: read newspaper, magazines, and books

▷ Looking at Language

POWER GRAMMAR

Past Tense

In English, when we talk about something that happened in the past, we use both the past tense (*got*) and a time expression (*yesterday*). It's easy to form regular past tense verbs (*look → looked*, *use → used*), but not always so easy to pronounce them. Depending on the pronunciation at the end of the verb (*t* in *want*, *d* in *end*), we add a syllable with –*ed* (*wanted*, *ended*) or not (*worked*, *watched*).

   With irregular verbs in the past tense, learning the form (*get → got*, *take → took*) is more difficult than pronouncing it. (See Appendix 3 for a list of common verbs that are irregular in the past tense.)

   In the negative, the past tense is easy: You simply say *didn't* + verb (*didn't get*, *didn't want*, *didn't use*).

Pronunciation: Regular Verbs

The past tense of most regular verbs is not pronounced clearly. It is only a quick *d* (first column) or *t* (second column) sound. With verbs already ending in the *t* or *d* sound, however, you add a syllable with –*ed* (third column). Listen to your teacher pronounce these verbs (syllable-stress pattern in parentheses):

/d/	/t/	/ed/
learn-learned [1-1]	work-worked [1-1]	want-wanted [2-1]
call-called [1-1]	reach-reached [1-1]	end-ended [2-1]
use-used [1-1]	walk-walked [1-1]	need-needed [2-1]
range-ranged [1-1]	look-looked [1-1]	add-added [2-1]
happen-happened [2-1]	miss-missed [1-1]	start-started [2-1]
study-studied [2-1]	call-called [1-1]	test-tested [2-1]
assume-assumed [2-2]	approach-approached [2-2]	visit-visited [3-1]

ACTIVITY **13** **Practicing the past tense**

Practice asking and answering the following questions with a partner.

1. Describe what happened on your first day at this school.
2. Tell me about an unforgettable test you took.
3. Tell me about your earliest memories of school.
4. Talk about a positive or negative experience in elementary school.

▷ Academic Speaking Task 2

Talking with a Professor about a Problem

When you have a problem with a class, you need to deal with it. The instructor may not be aware that something is wrong until you tell her or him, so the first step is to speak with the professor. If it's not possible to do so before or after class, make an appointment to see the professor some other time. One way to talk about a problem is to follow this sequence of steps:

1. Say what happened—just the facts—no opinions.
2. Say how it made you feel.
3. Tell the instructor what you want as a solution. Do it politely.
4. Listen to the reply. If no solution is offered, ask what the instructor can do to help you solve the problem.

Try not to get too emotional. If you get angry, for instance, the instructor may not listen to you. Stay calm and tell the truth. Most instructors are reasonable and want to be fair with their students.

If you are not satisfied with the explanation you receive, find out the school's policy for handling problems like yours. Ask someone in the department office, read information about school policies, or look on the college's website.

Example: You received a C for a final grade in a class, but your quiz and test grades average out to a B.

Excuse me, Professor. My name is Raul Lira. I was in your psychology class, and I had a question about my grade . . .
I received a C, but my test grades average out to a B. I'm confused. I think my grade should be a B.

ACTIVITY 14 Role-playing

Take turns playing the roles of student and instructor in the following scenarios. As the student, don't forget to follow the steps outlined above.

1. You handed in a paper that was three pages long; your classmate's paper was one page long. Your classmate got a higher grade than you did.
2. You had to work overtime and couldn't hand in an assignment on time. The instructor refused to accept your homework late.
3. On your test, the instructor deducted eight points for a question that was worth four points.
4. You got stuck in traffic and arrived late for a test, so you didn't have enough time to finish all the questions.
5. You think the instructor doesn't like you and treats you differently from the other students.
6. You were absent from class last week because you had to go to the airport to pick up relatives who came to visit you. The instructor didn't allow you to make up the quiz you missed.
7. You received an F on a paper for plagiarizing. You used the Internet to do research for the paper, but you didn't copy.

▷ Academic Speaking Task 3

Preparing and Giving a Short Presentation

In Chapter 4, you practiced three important presentation skills: eye contact, posture, and voice quality. In Chapter 5, you prepared and practiced a three-minute speech. In this chapter, you will prepare and present a short speech on your own, using the same guidelines as before. Review the steps and Do's and Don'ts on pages 142 and 180. In addition, you need to do the following:

Requirements

1. Choose a topic from the following list and speak three to five minutes;
2. Speak as naturally as possible, limiting your notes to one 3" × 5" card;
3. Make a handout for the audience with five to seven new words and their definitions;
4. Use at least one visual (a photograph, overhead transparency, drawing, or real object); and
5. Be prepared to answer three questions from the audience.

Topics

   a. Talk about an important lesson you learned from your parents.
   b. Tell a story about something you learned as a child.
   c. Describe the most difficult thing you ever learned to do.
   d. Talk about the most useful thing you learned in high school.
   e. Discuss something you have learned that is unique—that is, something most people don't know.

ACTIVITY 15 **Preparing an oral presentation**

Prepare a short oral presentation according to the requirements above. Bring your notes, handout, and/or visual to class.

ACTIVITY 16 **Practicing your speech**

Use your notes from Activity 15 to practice your speech.

   1. Sit facing a classmate.

      Student A: Give your speech.

      Student B: Listen and take notes. If something is not clear, ask a question.

   2. Move to another desk and practice with a different partner.

   3. Make any changes to your speech that you or your partner(s) think are necessary before speaking in front of the whole class.

Part 3

▷ Getting Ready for the Test: Self-Assessment

ACTIVITY 17 **Evaluating your skills**

Evaluate yourself on the following skills by putting a ✓ in the column that best describes how you feel you can do each. For every check in the third column, go back and practice before you take the test.

Listening I can:	Great	OK	Need to practice
1. understand some common phrasal verbs			
2. listen critically to new information			
3. understand & use new vocabulary			
4. listen for main ideas & then details			
5. understand expressions of equality (*as . . . as*)			

Speaking I am able to:	Great	OK	Need to practice
1. talk about research experiments, especially on learning (mice & mazes)			
2. use some inseparable phrasal verbs			
3. use *as . . . as* to express similarities & differences			
4. interpret a line graph			
5. use the simple past tense with correct pronunciation			
6. talk with a professor about a problem			
7. give a short oral presentation			
Study skills I should:			
1. make conclusions using inductive & deductive reasoning			
2. listen to a psychology lecture & take notes on my own			
3. use a variety of abbreviations & symbols in my notes			
4. be observant			
5. plan a short oral presentation			

▷ Chapter Test

To evaluate your progress, your instructor may ask you to do some or all of the following activities for the chapter test.

Listening Test Activities

ACTIVITY 18   **Listening and taking notes on your own**

Listen to the following mini-lecture and take notes, using abbreviations and symbols. Write your notes on a separate sheet of paper that you will hand in later.

ACTIVITY 19   **Using your notes to answer questions**

Using your notes from the mini-lecture in Activity 18, answer the questions you hear in complete sentences. Your instructor may ask you to answer orally.

1.

2.

3.

4.

5.

ACTIVITY **20** **Understanding phrasal verbs**

Listen to the sentences, and check (✓) the idea that is closest in meaning to what you hear.

You hear:

What have you come up with?

You check:

___✓___ What ideas did you think of?

_____ What work have you completed?

1. _____ Let's return to the study.

_____ Let's review the results of the study.

2. _____ Some mice in the maze never attracted attention.

_____ Some mice never reached the end of the maze.

3. _____ There were no more research mice.

_____ The researchers examined the mice.

4. _____ The data represent the control and experimental groups.

_____ There's a noticeable difference between the control and experimental groups.

5. _____ The researchers finished writing the data.

_____ The researchers reviewed the data.

Speaking Test Activities

ACTIVITY **21** **Interpreting a graph**

Answer questions about a graph from the chapter, or bring a graph from a magazine or local newspaper to talk about in class.

ACTIVITY **22** **Talking about the lecture**

Answer questions and talk about the lecture "Amazing Mice."

ACTIVITY 23 **Using the past tense**

Use the past tense to answer the questions your instructor asks you.

Speaking Evaluation Checklists

Your instructor may use the following checklists to assess your speaking in class activities and/or in the Speaking Test.

Speaking evaluation	OK	Needs work	Example(s)
Listening			
► understood question			
Content			
► answered correctly			
Language use			
► expressed ideas clearly			
► used language from chapter			
Pronunciation			
► clear & comprehensible			
► not too fast or slow			
► loud enough			
Nonverbal communication			
► appropriate eye contact			
► correct posture			

Oral presentation	OK	Needs work	Example(s)
Preparation			
► organized ideas			
► used notes effectively			
► explained new vocabulary			
► answered audience questions			
Language use			
► expressed ideas clearly			
► spoke naturally			
Pronunciation			
► comprehensible			
► not too fast or slow			
► loud enough			
Nonverbal communication			
► appropriate eye contact			
► correct posture & gestures			
► effective visuals			

WEB POWER

You will find additional exercises related to the content in this chapter at http://esl.college.hmco.com/students.

Appendix 1

▷ Chapter 1, "Cry Wolf"

ACTIVITY **7** **Using new vocabulary**

[Note to Student: If you are looking at this page, your partner should be looking at page 7.]

Example: What century were you born in?

1. Did Aesop live around 600AD?
2. If you have a personal problem you need help with, what do you ask your friends for?
3. How do you feel when you're really, really scared?
4. What do you call the people in a book or movie?

[Now switch roles. Turn to page 7.]

5. If my watch is five minutes slow, it's not *what*?
6. A period of ten years is a decade. What do you call a period of 100 years?
7. If something is different from all others, how would you describe it?
8. If I say someone is honest and shy, I've given you two *what*?

ACTIVITY 19   Asking questions about language

[Note to Student: If you are looking at this page, your partner should have her or his book closed. Ask the first three questions and then switch roles.]

> **Example:** You know how to say the word "unique," but you don't know how to write it.

1. You see a name in your humanities textbook; it's spelled P-l-a-t-o. You never heard the name spoken. What do you ask?
2. It's Friday afternoon, and you say that this weekend you're going to make a party. Your teacher corrects you and says, "No, you're not going to **make** a party—you're going to **have** a party." What question do you ask about *make* and *do*?
3. Your writing teacher gives back your homework. She underlined in red the word b-e-l-e-i-v-e. What do you ask?

[Now switch roles. Close your book.]

4. You're not sure about a word your classmate is using. He keeps saying, "That fable illustrates blah-blah-blah," but you don't really understand what he means by "illustrate." What question do you ask?
5. You don't remember a word from the lecture, but you know that the professor used it when talking about Aesop and whether he really lived or not. What do you ask?
6. You're writing a paragraph about Aesop, and you don't know if you should use the word *dead* or *died*. What question do you ask?

◢ Chapter 2, "Food Chains"

ACTIVITY 8   Using academic words

[Note to Student: If you are looking at this page, your partner should be looking at pages 46–47.]

> **Example:** What do you call a person who cares about the environment?

1. What's another way to say *as a result*?
2. How do we describe a problem related to the water we drink and/or the air we breathe?

3. When a word has more than one meaning, we say that it has several what?
4. What's a synonym for *idea*?

[Now switch roles. Turn to page 48.]

5. What does *ID* stand for?
6. What word means "one part in one hundred"?
7. What do plants get from the sun and humans get from food?
8. Getting a college degree is a long and complicated what?

▷ Chapter 3, "Forbidden Food"

ACTIVITY 8   Using academic vocabulary

[Note to Student: If you are reading from this page, your partner should be looking at pages 82–84 for the answer. Switch after the first four.]

Example: For both Muslims and Jews, eating pork is . . .

Finish the following sentences:

1. A cat is not a wild animal like a tiger. It's . . .
2. I didn't sleep last night, and I haven't eaten today. I feel tired and I have no . . .
3. I'm sorry. The restaurant is full. There are no tables . . .
4. If you want to know how much beer people consume every year, you need to go on the Internet and search for "annual beer . . ."

[Now switch roles. Turn to page 83.]

5. The plus sign and the minus sign are both mathematical . . .
6. One law in physics is that for every action, there is a . . .
7. Children under the age of seventeen cannot see R-rated movies. It is . . .
8. If a student with a C grade-point average applies to Stanford or Harvard University, that student will not be accepted. He or she will be . . .

ACTIVITY 14 Reading numbers in a table

[Note to Student: If you are looking at the table on this page, your partner should be looking at pages 90–91.]

Face your partner and ask questions to complete the information in Table 1.

Look at Table 1 to answer your partner's questions.

Example 1: *What was the per capita meat consumption in the United States in 1993? (Listen and write the answer.)*

Example 2: *(Your partner reads from page 90)*

Table 1

Consumption trends of meat, past and projected to the year 2020					
Region	**Per capita meat consumption (kg)**			**Annual growth of meat consumption (percent/year) 1982–1993**	**Projected annual growth of meat consumption (percent/year) 1993–2020**
	1983	**1993**	**2020**		
United States	107		114	1.8	0.6
China	16	33	63		3.2
India	4	4	7	3.1	3.3
Other East Asia	22	44	70		2.6
Other South Asia	6	7	10	5.4	3.3
Southeast Asia	11		28	5.4	
Latin America	40	46	57	3.2	2.2
WANA	20	20	23	2.6	2.7
Sub-Saharan Africa	10		11	2.1	3.4
Developing world	15	21	31	5.3	2.9
Developed world	74	78	81	1.2	0.5
World	30	34	40	2.8	1.8

"Meat" includes beef, pork, mutton and goat, and poultry. WANA is Western Asia and North Africa.

ACTIVITY **17**   Answering questions about a table

[Note to Student: If you are reading from this page, your partner should be looking at page 91 for the answer. Don't forget to write down the answers your partner gives.]

> **Example:** What was the meat consumption of Latin America in 1983?

1. What is the projected meat consumption of China in the year 2020?
2. Which country had a faster growth of meat consumption from 1982 to 1993, China or the United States?
3. Compare the amount of meat an Indian ate in the year 1993 with the amount another South Asian ate in the same year. Was it a little more? A lot more? A little less? Or a lot less?
4. According to the table, who eats the most meat?
5. The projected growth of meat consumption in China is 3.2% per year, which is less than that of Southeast Asia. Which represents a higher amount of meat? Why?

[Now switch roles. Turn to page 91.]

6. What was the meat consumption of the developed world in 1993?
7. How much meat does a person in Canada eat compared to someone who lives in Somalia? (A little more/less? A lot more/less?)
8. What's the average annual growth of meat consumption from 1982 to 1993?
9. According to the table, who eats the least amount of meat?
10. From 1993 to 2020, which part of the world will have the slowest rate of growth in the consumption of meat?

ACTIVITY **18**   Reading URLs and e-mail addresses

[Note to Student: If you are on this page, your partner should have her or his book closed. She or he should write what you say.]

> **Example:** *terry, T-E-R-R-Y, dot aki, A-K-I, at mindspring dot com*

1. http://www.buddhanet.net/
2. http://chinesefood.about.com/cs/foodculture/a/unusualfood.htm
3. tom_ahl@usu.edu

4. kim.chee@yahoo.com
5. http://www.ent.iastate.edu/misc/insectsasfood.html

[Now switch roles. Close your book.]

6. http://www.jewfaq.org/kashrut.htm
7. http://www.ifanca.org/halal.htm
8. juan.ton@yahoo.com
9. sue_shea@mac.com
10. http://www.hinduwebsite.com/hinduism/h_food.htm

[Now check each other's answers.]

▷ Chapter 4, "Bacteria Burgers"

ACTIVITY 9   Using academic words

[Note to Student: If you are on this page, your partner should be on page 121.]

Example: If there's a dangerous problem with a new product, what does the company have to do?

1. If you get better after you've been sick, what have you done?
2. If you put money or time into something, what is this action called?
3. If you take something apart to see how it works, what are you doing?
4. If an airplane crashes, what does the government conduct in order to find out the cause?

[Now switch roles. Turn to page 120.]

5. What kind of facility takes cows and converts them into beef?
6. What kind of analysis involves money?
7. When you direct an experiment or an investigation, what are you doing?
8. When things happen in a certain order, what do you call it?

ACTIVITY 17   Reading and talking about equations

[Note to Student: If you are on this page, your partner should be on page 135.]

Example: Seven times six equals forty-two.

1. Twenty-four times three equals seventy-two.
2. One hundred seventeen plus seventy equals one hundred eighty-seven.
3. Six hundred eighty-two divided by three hundred forty-one equals two.
4. Three-fourths minus five-eighths equals one-eighth.
5. What's four point three three minus three point two three?

[Switch roles. Turn to page 135.]

6. Two hundred thirteen divided by three equals seventy-one.
7. One and a half plus one half equals two.
8. Seven thousand six hundred forty minus fourteen hundred equals six thousand two hundred forty.
9. Seventy-eight times seven equals five hundred forty-six.
10. What's one point five two plus three point oh seven?

[Now check each other's answers.]

ACTIVITY **18** **Reading fractions and percentages**

[Note to Student: If you are on this page, your partner should be on page 138.]

    Example: One kilo is the same as two point two pounds.

1. More than ¾ of the illnesses due to food are caused by unknown sources.
2. Among the illnesses due to food, 30% are caused by bacteria, 3% by parasites, and 67% by viruses.
3. More than ⅘ of the illnesses caused by the dangerous kind of *E. coli* are transmitted through food.
4. Only 5% of the people who are infected with *E. coli* report it, whereas ⅓ of the hepatitis A cases are reported.

[Switch roles. Turn to page 138.]

5. Bacteria cause 72% of the deaths associated with food poisoning, but only ¹⁄₁₀ of the hospitalizations for stomach problems are due to bacteria.
6. Infections with other types of *E. coli* bacteria are ½ as common as those with *E. coli* 0157:H7.
7. 5 microorganisms are the cause of more than 90% of the estimated food-related deaths. *E. coli* is one of them, causing 3% of these deaths.
8. Approximately .7% of the estimated 76 million annual cases of food poisoning in the United States are caused by *E. coli*. That's ⁷⁄₁₀ of 1%.

[Now check each other's answers.]

▷ Chapter 5, "Canine Colleagues"

ACTIVITY 8 Using academic words

[Note to Student: If you are looking at this page, your partner should be looking at pages 164–165 for the answer.]

Finish the following sentences:

> **Example:** Administrators want to know how well their instructors are doing in the classroom, so they ask the students to fill out an instructor . . .

1. If smoking is banned somewhere, in other words, you can't smoke there, then smoking is . . .
2. Charles Darwin, who traveled to the Galápagos Islands and observed species of plants and animals there, is famous for his theory of . . .
3. You really helped me out yesterday. Thank-you for your . . .
4. You need to fill out that form and turn it in to the Social Security . . .

[Now switch roles. Turn to pages 164–165.]

Finish the following sentences:

5. This website is confusing; it's hard to read and it's not clear. The colors are too dark, and the print is too small. I don't like the . . .
6. In every job, the boss wants to know the quality of the employees' work, and the employees want to know how they are doing on the job, so they go through some kind of . . .
7. Put away that gun! Don't you know that guns are . . .
8. Could you please tell me how to turn this off? I need some . . .

▷ Chapter 6, "Amazing Mice"

ACTIVITY 8   Using academic words

[Note to Student: If you are reading from this page, your partner should be looking at pages 207–208 for the answer. Switch after the first four.]

> **Example:** How did you deal with the problem—objectively or subjectively?

Answer the following questions:

1. How would you describe thinking that follows the rules of deductive or inductive reasoning?
2. If the youngest person in an experiment is 22 years old, and the oldest is 76, what do you call the difference between their ages?
3. If you see a wedding ring on a person's ring finger, what do you automatically think?
4. What do you call this: 2, 4, 8, 16, 32, 64 . . . ?

[Now switch roles. Turn to pages 207–208.]

Answer the following questions:

5. If you locked your keys in the house and couldn't enter the house through the windows or door, you would have to try a different what?
6. What would you call this: If $a > b$, then $b > a$?
7. What's another word for *series*?
8. Learning another language well involves a lot of things: time, study, practice, your personality and ability . . . What do you call all these things that affect your learning?

ACTIVITY 11 Using *as . . . as*

[Note to Student: If you are reading from this page, your partner should have her or his book closed. Switch after the first five.]

Example: Natasha studies a little. Kim studies a lot.

1. Natasha's GPA (grade point average) is 2.8. Kim's is 3.8.
2. Natasha's taking fifteen credits. Kim is also taking fifteen credits this semester.
3. Natasha is doing well in Psych 101. Kim is not doing well in Psych 101.
4. Kim works hard, and Natasha does, too.
5. Kim spent $180 on her textbooks. Natasha spent $140 on hers.

[Now switch roles. Close your book.]

6. Last semester Natasha's classes were fairly easy. This semester her classes are hard.
7. Kim has a little homework. Natasha has a lot of homework.
8. Kim has one assignment. Natasha has four.
9. Kim's tuition is higher this year than it was last year.
10. There are a lot of cute guys in Natasha's biology class, but just a few in her psych class.

Appendix 2

▷ The Language of Math

Cardinal Numbers

0	zero	42	forty-two
1	one	50	fifty
2	two	53	fifty-three
3	three	60	sixty
4	four	64	sixty-four
5	five	70	seventy
6	six	75	seventy-five
7	seven	80	eighty
8	eight	86	eighty-six
9	nine	90	ninety
10	ten	97	ninety-seven
11	eleven	100	one hundred (a hundred)
12	twelve	200	two hundred
13	thirteen	300	three hundred
14	fourteen	1,000	one thousand (a thousand)
15	fifteen	4,000	four thousand
16	sixteen	5,000	five thousand
17	seventeen	10,000	ten thousand
18	eighteen	11,000	eleven thousand
19	nineteen	56,000	fifty-six thousand
20	twenty	100,000	one hundred thousand
21	twenty-one		(a hundred thousand)
22	twenty-two	1,000,000	one million (a million)
23	twenty-three	10,000,000	ten million
24	twenty-four	100,000,000	one hundred million
25	twenty-five		(a hundred million)
30	thirty	1,000,000,000	one billion (a billion)
40	forty	1,000,000,000,000	one trillion (a trillion)

Ordinal Numbers

1st	first		22nd	twenty-second
2nd	second		23rd	twenty-third
3rd	third		24th	twenty-fourth
4th	fourth		25th	twenty-fifth
5th	fifth		30th	thirtieth
6th	sixth		31st	thirty-first
7th	seventh		40th	fortieth
8th	eighth		42nd	forty-second
9th	ninth		50th	fiftieth
10th	tenth		53rd	fifty-third
11th	eleventh		60th	sixtieth
12th	twelfth		64th	sixty-fourth
13th	thirteenth		70th	seventieth
14th	fourteenth		75th	seventy-fifth
15th	fifteenth		80th	eightieth
16th	sixteenth		86th	eighty-sixth
17th	seventeenth		97th	ninety-seventh
18th	eighteenth		100th	one hundredth
19th	nineteenth		101st	one hundred (and) first
20th	twentieth		202nd	two hundred (and) second
21st	twenty-first		303rd	three hundred (and) third

Roman Numerals

I	one	XXII	twenty-two
II	two	XXV	twenty-five
III	three	XXX	thirty
IV	four	XL	forty
V	five	XLVI	forty-six
VI	six	L	fifty
VII	seven	LVIII	fifty-eight
VIII	eight	LX	sixty
IX	nine	LXX	seventy
X	ten	LXXX	eighty
XI	eleven	XC	ninety
XII	twelve	C	one hundred
XIII	thirteen	CC	two hundred
XIV	fourteen	CCC	three hundred
XV	fifteen	CD	four hundred
XVI	sixteen	D	five hundred
XVII	seventeen	DC	six hundred
XVIII	eighteen	DCC	seven hundred
XIX	nineteen	M	one thousand
XX	twenty	MM	two thousand

Appendix 3

Common Irregular Verbs

These verbs are grouped according to their pronunciation in the past tense. See pronunciation note in parentheses ( ).

Group 1	Past Tense (No change)
bet	bet
cost	cost
cut	cut
hit	hit
hurt	hurt
let	let
put	put
quit	quit
set	set
shut	shut
spread	spread

Group 2	Past Tense (final d→t)
bend	bent
build	built
lend	lent
send	sent
spend	spent

Group 3	Past Tense (ĕ)
fall	fell
feed	fed
feel	felt
hold	held
keep	kept
lead	led
leave	left
mean	meant
meet	met
read	read
say	said
sleep	slept
sweep	swept

Group 4	Past Tense (ō)
break	broke
choose	chose
drive	drove
freeze	froze
ride	rode
sell	sold
speak	spoke
steal	stole
tell	told
wake	woke
write	wrote

Group 5	Past Tense (o͝o)
shake	shook
take	took
(under)stand	(under)stood

Group 6	Past Tense (o͞o)
blow	blew
draw	drew
fly	flew
grow	grew
know	knew
throw	threw

Group 7	Past Tense (ô)
bring	brought
buy	bought
catch	caught
fight	fought
lose	lost
see	saw
teach	taught
tear	tore
think	thought
wear	wore

Group 8	Past Tense (ā)
become	became
come	came
eat	ate
give	gave
make	made
pay	paid

Group 9	Past Tense (ă)
begin	began
drink	drank
have	had
ring	rang
run	ran
sing	sang
sink	sank
sit	sat
swim	swam

Group 10	Past Tense (Variable)
be	was, were
bite	bit
hide	hid
do	did
find	found
for(get)	for(got)
shoot	shot
go	went
hang	hung
hear	heard
stick	stuck
win	won